·新体验商务英语系列教材·

商务英语函电与合同

International Business Correspondence and Contract

（修订本）

主　编　束光辉
副主编　东　刚

清华大学出版社
北京交通大学出版社
·北京·

内 容 简 介

本书共15个单元,主要内容包括:商务英语函电的文体、结构和格式,与对方建立商务关系函,询购函,报价函,订购与确认函,付款函,催款函,包装函,装运函,保险函,投诉索赔函,代理函,以及合同等。本书中所有的信函文本均来自进出口贸易实务的各个环节,同时文本的选择还兼顾了商务英语函电的得体性。本书所收录的信样较为详尽,而且种类丰富、新颖实用、写作风格多样,能够让学生学到真实的商务英语函电写作技巧。同时,本书对各种写作技巧的介绍也非常详尽,并且均采用国外较新的商务英语函电写作材料并体现了国内商务英语函电的写作特点。此外,本书还对这些信函及文本的典型句式进行了提炼和总结,有利于学生更好地掌握和应用。

本书可供英语专业学生、商务英语专业学生及具有较好英语基础的其他经贸专业学生作为教材使用,同时也可用作从事相关工作人员的自学用书及参考用书。

本书封面贴有清华大学出版社防伪标签,无标签者不得销售。
版权所有,侵权必究。侵权举报电话:010-62782989　13501256678　13801310933

图书在版编目(CIP)数据

商务英语函电与合同/束光辉主编.—修订本.—北京:北京交通大学出版社:清华大学出版社,2016.4(2021.2修订)

ISBN 978-7-5121-1825-6

Ⅰ.①商…　Ⅱ.①束…　Ⅲ.①国际贸易-英语-电报信函-写作　②国际贸易-英语-合同-写作　Ⅳ.①H315

中国版本图书馆CIP数据核字(2014)第020393号

商务英语函电与合同
SHANGWU YINGYU HANDIAN YU HETONG

责任编辑:	张利军
出版发行:	清 华 大 学 出 版 社　邮编:100084　电话:010-62776969
	北京交通大学出版社　邮编:100044　电话:010-51686414
印 刷 者:	北京时代华都印刷有限公司
经　　销:	全国新华书店
开　　本:	185 mm×260 mm　印张:15.25　字数:380千字
版 印 次:	2021年2月第1版第1次修订　2021年2月第4次印刷
印　　数:	6 001～8 000册　定价:42.00元

本书如有质量问题,请向北京交通大学出版社质监组反映。对您的意见和批评,我们表示欢迎和感谢。
投诉电话:010-51686043,51686008;传真:010-62225406;E-mail:press@bjtu.edu.cn。

进入21世纪，随着全球经济一体化进程的加快，我国与世界的经贸联系更加紧密，贸易形式更趋多元化。与此相伴的是，中国的商务英语教学与研究也发生了巨大的变化。这至少表现在以下几个方面：第一，如今，商务英语已是一个相当大的概念，它已从最早的一门单一的"外贸英语函电"课程发展到了涉及金融、保险、国际企业管理、国际经济法、海外投资与企业合作等多领域的学科；第二，人们对商务英语学习的需求持续旺盛，不仅几乎全国所有的高校都开设了商务英语专业或课程，而且越来越多的企业在职人员也迫切需要学习商务英语；第三，外语界对商务英语的研究也提高到了一个新的层次。

为了适应新的形势，许多高校都正在对一些传统的经贸英语类课程进行调整、改革和扩充，以培养新型的国际商务专业人才。这就向教材建设提出了更高的要求。教材不仅是教学内容的表现，更体现了人才培养的规格。纵观过去的一些教材，我们便不难发现，无论从内容上还是体例上，它们都已远远落后于当今国际经贸发展的形势，例如大多围绕语法、词汇和翻译等来展开，缺乏商务英语专业的实践性和语言的真实性，难以满足工作的需要。而另一些教材则又过于突出"专业"的内容，把商务英语教材混同于国际商务专业教材。因此，编写能够适应时代要求的国际商务英语教材显得尤为重要。正是在这样的背景下，由束光辉老师主编的"新体验商务英语系列教材"面世了，它体现了"贴近时代，融合语言与专业"的编写理念，是一次积极而大胆的尝试。

该系列包括《进出口贸易实务》《现代商务英语写作》《商务英语函电与合同》《商务报刊选读》《商务英语汉英翻译教程》《跨文化商务沟通》等教材。它们在内容设计和编写形式上具有以下特点。

1. 融专业性与语言技能于一体

该系列教材在编写上突出了以培养学生的实际工作能力为目标的思路，所选材料涉及了商务环境的各个方面，均能反映出商务工作实践性的特点，同时也体现了语言技能系统化培养的理念。该系列教材通过拟定各种商务环境，将商务知识和语言技能融合在一起，使学生的语言应用能力在更接近于真实的商务实践中得以提高。

2. 选材新，贴近时代

该系列教材在材料选择上参考了国内外最近几年出版的教材和其他相关材料，充分吸收了国内外最新的教学科研成果，体现了国际商务活动不断变化的特点和商务领域专业性的特点，具有鲜明的时代特征。同时，该系列教材的许多文本、范例和研究材料均来自于近年来各类商务实践，体现了商务英语的真实性和实践性。

3. 练习形式多样，针对性强

该系列教材的练习将语言技能训练与商务环境较好地结合在一起，通过各种题型，对所涉及的商务环节和领域，有针对性地对学生进行训练。这不仅能够巩固学生所学的专业知识，而且还将提高他们的语言技能。

21 世纪的中国更加开放，更加开放的中国在诸多方面都在与世界接轨。作为国际商务沟通的一个重要工具，商务英语的教学和研究理应跟上时代的发展和社会的需求。我们要更加重视并加强对商务英语教学的研究。该系列教材的编写是一次很好的探索，希望借此能进一步提高我国高校商务英语的教学和科研水平，为培养我国新型国际商务专业人才做出贡献。

中国国际贸易学会
国际商务英语研究委员会
原副主任
2021 年 2 月

前言

商务函电写作是从事国际贸易工作者必备的业务技能之一，它涉及国际贸易实务、惯例、相关国家的风俗文化及语言修辞等诸多方面。本书包括下列内容：商务英语函电的文体、结构和格式，与对方建立商务关系函、询购函、报价函、订购与确认函、付款函、催款函、包装函、装运函、保险函、投诉索赔函、代理函，以及合同等。本书几乎全部用英文编写。所有信函文本均来自进出口贸易实务的各个环节，同时文本的选择还兼顾了商务英语函电的得体性，在用词方面做到不卑不亢，应宽时宽、应严时严，表现了文本作者的写作目的和所期望达到的效果。本书所收录的信样较为详尽，而且种类丰富、新颖实用、写作风格多样，能够让学生学到真实的商务英语函电写作技巧。同时，本书对各种写作技巧的介绍也非常详尽，并且均采用国外较新的商务英语函电写作材料并体现了国内商务英语函电的写作特点。此外，本书还对这些信函及文本的典型句式进行了提炼和总结，有利于学生更好地掌握和应用。

本书的另一个特点是，它克服了国内教材重语言形式、轻语言运用能力之弊端，突出学生商务英语函电写作交际能力的培养，通过拟定国际贸易实务的有关环节，让学生有针对性地进行写作训练，以使他们的写作更具有真实性和得体性。

本书的主要读者对象为英语专业学生、商务英语专业学生及具有较好英语基础的其他经贸专业学生，同时也可用作从事相关工作人员的自学用书及参考用书。

本书由束光辉担任主编，东刚担任副主编。其中，束光辉编写了第1、2、7、8、9、10、11、12、13单元的课文、练习及本书的所有附录，东刚编写了第3、4、5、6、14单元的课文和练习。

本书的编写与出版得到了北京交通大学语言与传播学院领导的大力支持及北京交通大学出版社张利军编辑的热情帮助，在此一并表示衷心的感谢。

编　者

2021年2月

Contents

Unit 1 An Overview of Business Letter Writing
商务信函写作概览 ·· (1)
1.1 The Principles for Effective Writing ··· (1)
1.2 The Style and Tone of Business Letter Writing ····································· (7)
1.3 Preparation before Writing ··· (8)
1.4 Writing Naturally and Sincerely ··· (9)

Unit 2 The Structure and Styles of Business Letters
商务信函的结构与格式 ·· (15)
2.1 Principal Parts ·· (15)
2.2 Optional Elements ·· (18)
2.3 Styles of a Business Letter ··· (19)
2.4 Spacing, Margin and Envelop Addressing ··· (23)

Unit 3 Establishing Business Relations
与对方建立商务关系 ··· (29)
3.1 Introduction ·· (29)
3.2 Letter Samples ·· (30)

Unit 4 Inquiries
询购 ··· (42)
4.1 Introduction ·· (42)
4.2 Letter Samples ·· (43)

Unit 5 Quotations, Offers and Counter Offers
报盘与还盘 ··· (53)
5.1 Quotations and Offers ·· (53)
5.2 Counter Offers ·· (59)

I

Unit 6 Orders and Acknowledgements
订购与确认 ·· (71)
6.1　Introduction ·· (71)
6.2　Letter Samples ··· (72)

Unit 7 Payment by Letter of Credit
信用证付款 ··· (86)
7.1　Introduction ·· (86)
7.2　Letter Samples ··· (87)

Unit 8 Other Methods of Payment
其他付款方式 ·· (99)
8.1　Introduction of Other Methods of Payment ·································· (99)
8.2　Writing for Other Methods of Payment ······································ (100)
8.3　Letter Samples ·· (100)

Unit 9 Collection Letters
催款函 ··· (112)
9.1　Introduction ··· (112)
9.2　Letter Samples ·· (115)

Unit 10 Packing
包装 ·· (126)
10.1　Introduction ·· (126)
10.2　Letter Samples ··· (127)

Unit 11 Shipping
装运 ·· (136)
11.1　Introduction ·· (136)
11.2　Letter samples ··· (137)

Unit 12 Insurance
保险 ·· (148)
12.1　Introduction ·· (148)
12.2　Letter Samples ··· (149)

Unit 13 Complaints and Claims
投诉与索赔 ·· (160)
13.1　Introduction ·· (160)

  13.2 Letter Samples ··· (161)

Unit 14 Agency
    代理 ·· (174)
  14.1 Introduction ·· (174)
  14.2 Letter Samples ··· (175)

Unit 15 Contracts
    合同 ·· (188)
  15.1 Types of Business Contracts ·· (188)
  15.2 Components of a Business Contract ······································ (190)
  15.3 Language and Stylistics Features ·· (190)
  15.4 Layout ·· (193)
  15.5 Writing Steps ··· (193)

Appendix A Useful Abbreviations in International Trade
      实用国际贸易缩略语 ··· (212)

Appendix B Useful Expressions in INCOTERMS 2010 and the Relevant Documents
      《2010年国际贸易术语解释通则》及相关文件中的实用表达 ············ (218)

Appendix C The Comparison of the Old and New Language Styles
      新旧文体比较 ··· (231)

References
  参考文献 ·· (234)

Unit 1

An Overview of Business Letter Writing
商务信函写作概览

It is a valuable business asset to be able to write effectively. One reason is that a great deal of business is conducted via writing. With the wide use of fax and recent development of EDI, more and more writing is involved in every part of business. Another reason is that effective business letter writer can use their writing skill to help increase their company's sales and profits by building up good relations with customers, employees, and the public. In addition, proficiency in writing gives the man or woman in business a personal advantage over less capable writers and contributes substantially to his or her self-confidence, which is a necessary quality for business success.

1.1 The Principles for Effective Writing

In your English business letter writing, you need to learn and apply certain principles to effectively communicating with others. These writing principles can be summed up as 7Cs, i. e. Completeness, Clearness, Conciseness, Consideration, Courtesy, Concreteness and Correctness.

1.1.1 Completeness

A practical English writing is very successful and highly effective well only when it contains all the necessary information to the readers (the counterpart or the public) and answers all the questions and requirements put forward by the readers. See to it that all the matters are stated or discussed, and all the questions are answered or explained.[1] For instance, when the buyers write a letter to accept an offer that the sellers made, the buyers must state his condition of acceptance in detail or quote the evidences of the offer.

In order to verify the completeness of what you write, five "Ws" (who, what, where, when and why) and one "h" (how) should be used. For example, if what you write is a letter of order, you should make it clear that who wants to order, what he wants, when he needs the goods, where the goods to be sent and how payment will be made. If some special requirements should be presented, you could explain why you would do so.

1.1.2 Clearness

Clarity tells the reader exactly what he or she wants and needs to know, using words and a format that make your writings totally understood with just one reading. To achieve this, you should include illustrations, examples or visual aids to convey your information, and, above all, use simple, plain language and avoid business jargons.

Basically, the writer should keep off anything that might be misleading or avoid using the words, and sentences that are equivocal in meaning.[2] To meet such an end, the writer should follow the following rules.

(1) Try to use the concise and accessible expressions.

Let us look at the following sentence:

As to the steamer sailing from Shanghai to Los Angeles, we have bimonthly direct services.

The basic meaning of this sentence is "we have direct sailings from Shanghai to Los Angels", but the word "bimonthly" has two meanings, one of which is "twice a month" and the other of which is "once every two months". You'd better not use the word like "bimonthly" of double meanings, but use the words that can express your idea clearly as follows:

① We have a direct sailing from Shanghai to Los Angeles every two months.

② We have a direct sailing from Shanghai to Los Angeles semimonthly.

③ We have two direct sailings every month from Shanghai to Los Angeles.

(2) Pay attention to the position of modifier.

The basic principle for using modifiers is simply to put them as close as possible to the word or words they are modifying. Naturally, if you want to discuss *a potential market*, you will want *potential* to appear right before *market*; you will not put the modifier in some distant part of the sentence.

The idea of keeping related words together — and as close together as possible — is probably the "whole idea" behind studying modifiers.[3] Adjectives should be placed right next to the things they describe and adverbs should be placed right next to the action or the other modifiers they describe.

Let us look at the following sentences:

Your proposal for payment by time draft is acceptable to us under Order No. 115.

This sentence is poor in that "under Order No. 115" is too far away from payment by time draft.

(3) Pay attention to the object of the pronoun and the relations between the relative pronoun and the antecedent.

Whom or what the pronoun refers to and what is the relation between the relative pronoun and the antecedent? These should be paid attention to. Generally speaking, the pronoun and relative pronoun are used to refer to the nearest noun from themselves and should be identical in person and number with the noun referred to or modified. Let us examine the following sentence:

They informed Messrs. Smith & Brown that they would receive a reply in a few days.

In this sentence, what does the second "they" refer to, the subject "They" of the main clause or the "Messrs. Smith & Brown"? This can't be explained clearly. It will be clear if you change the sentence into:

They informed Messrs. Smith & Brown that the latter would receive the reply in a few days.

(4) Pay attention to the rationality in logic.

At first, you must pay attention to the agreement of the logical subject of the participle and the subject of the sentence. For example:

Being a registered accountant, I'm sure you can help us.

In this sentence, the subject of the sentence is "I", but the logical subject of the participle "being" should be "you" according to inference. In order to keep the logical subject of the participle in agreement with the subject of the sentence, the above sentence should be rewritten as the following:

① Being a registered accountant, you can certainly help us.
② As you are a registered accountant, I'm sure you can help us.

1.1.3 Conciseness

Conciseness is considered the most important principle in business letter writing as we now live in a world where time is money. Conciseness means to write in the fewest possible worlds without sacrificing completeness and courtesy. To achieve conciseness, you should avoid wordy statement and fancy language, use short sentences instead of long ones, and compose your message carefully. To achieve this, the following guidelines must be adhered to.

(1) Make a long story short and try to avoid wordiness.

Make it a rule, to use no more words and pithy sentences to express your meaning clearly and concisely. Try to use a word or phrase to express your idea as much as possible instead of using long sentences or clauses. For instance:

You shouldn't use:	You'd better use:
at this time	now
express a preference for	prefer
enclosed herewith	here

from the point of view	as
in view of the fact that	because

(2) Avoid the unusual or out-of-date words or jargons and try to express your idea in modern English.

You shouldn't use:	You'd better use:
consummate	complete
terminate	end
remuneration	payment
converse	talk
inst	this month
attached hereto	enclosed is/are
acknowledge receipt of	thank you for ... I received ...
awaiting the favor of our early reply	we are looking forward to your reply
up to this writing	so far
Take the liberty of	omitted

(3) Build effective sentences and paragraphs.

Generally speaking, the average length for sentences should be 10 to 20 words, not over 30 ones. Usually a paragraph consists of no more than 10 lines because short paragraphs encourage the readers to finish reading over the passage.

Let us look at the following sentence:

We would like to know whether you would allow us to extend the time of shipment for twenty days and if you would be so kind as to allow us to do so, kindly give us your reply by fax without delay.

This sentence is a bit lengthy, and is too courteous in expressions, which sounds unclear in meaning. In order to express the main idea better, this sentence may be abbreviated as follows:

Please reply by fax immediately if you will allow us to delay the shipment until April 21.

1.1.4 Consideration

Consideration means thoughtfulness. So you should always put yourself in your reader's place, which is what people now emphasize, i. e. "You" attitude, and avoid taking the writer's attitude, i. e. "We" attitude. Therefore, you should always keep in mind the receiver we are writing to, understand his or her problems and take the positive approach.

Let's make a comparison between the following two groups of sentences.

"We" attitude	"You" attitude
We allow a 5% discount for cash payment.	You earn a 5% discount when you pay cash.

In addition, we should try to discuss problems in a positive way rather than in a negative way. Make a comparison between the following groups of sentences and you will find which is better.

(1) a. We do not believe that you will have cause for dissatisfaction. (Negative)
    b. We feel sure that you will entirely get satisfied. (Positive)

(2) a. Your order will be delayed for two weeks (Negative)
    b. Your order will be shipped in two weeks (Positive)

1.1.5 Courtesy

Review of actual business correspondence reveals that special attention should be devoted to assuming the courtesy of business communication.[4] By courtesy we mean treating people with respect and friendly human concern. Effective writers visualize the reader before starting to write.[5] They consider the reader's desires, problems, circumstances, emotions and probable reactions to their request. Let us compare the following sentences.

(1) We are sorry that you misunderstood us.
(2) We are sorry that we did not make ourselves clear.

In Sentence (1), the party of the author is to put the blame on the customer for something, but in Sentence (2), the party of the author takes the initiative to bear the responsibility.

There are a lot of language styles or ways to express courtesy, some of which will be presented here for your reference as follows:

(1) Change the commanding tone into requesting tone, that is, change the imperative sentence into general question with the word "will" or "would" at the beginning. For example:

① Will you tell us detailed information on your requirements?
② Will you please tell us more detailed information on your requirements?
③ Would you please tell us more detailed information on your requirements?

(2) Use the past subjunctive form.

① Would you send us your latest catalogues and price lists on cotton piece goods?
② We would ask you to make a prompt shipment.
③ We wish you would let us have your reply soon.

(3) Use mitigation and avoid overemphasizing your own opinion or irritating your partner.

In order to avoid overemphasizing your own opinion and irritating your partner, you should use mitigation, such as: We are afraid that ..., We would say ..., It seems to us that ..., We would suggest that ..., etc.

(4) Passive voice should be adopted accordingly.

In some cases, passive voice appears more courteous than active voice because it can avoid blaming the doer of the act. For example:

① You made a very careless mistake during the course of shipment.

② A very careless mistake was made during the course of shipment.

① You did not enclose the price list in you letter

② The price list was not enclosed in your letter.

(5) Try to avoid using the words with forcing tone or arousing unpleasantness.

Some words or expressions such as "demand", "disgust", "refuse", "want you to" will arouse unpleasant feeling in audience, therefore they should be avoided or changed into some forms to express. Let us look at the following examples.

① We demand prompt shipment from you.

② We request prompt shipment from you.

① We must refuse your offer.

② We regret that we are unable to accept your offer.

(6) Use expressions about joy and willingness, thanks and regret, etc.

① It is with pleasure that we have reached an agreement on all the terms.

② It is a pleasure for us to sign such a sales contract.

③ Thank you for your letter of July 9th, 2015.

④ We are extremely sorry that we could not answer your letter in due time.

1.1.6 Concreteness

Business writing should be vivid, specific and definite rather than vague, general and abstract, especially when the writer is requiring a response, solving problems, making an offer or acceptance, etc.[6] We need to use specific facts, figures and time to stress concreteness, for they can help write concretely and vividly. Let us look at the following sentences:

We wish to confirm our fax dispatched yesterday.

Like today and tomorrow, the word yesterday is a vague and general concept, which allows possibility for misinterpretation.

1.1.7 Correctness

Correct spelling, proper grammar and punctuation will give your letter a good appearance but they are not all the factors that correctness comprises. In our business letters, you should attach great importance to this writing principle, especially when you are giving information regarding dates, specifications, prices, quantities, discounts, commission, units and figures, etc. A minor mistake in this respect sometimes means you will make no profit or even lose out. Let us look at the following sentences to see if there are anything improper.

(1) All offers by fax are open for 5 days.

The above sentence does not clearly explain or account for specific 5 days, and should be changed into:

All offers by fax are open for 5 days inclusive of the date of dispatch.

(2) This contract will come into effect from Oct. 1.

The above sentence does not clearly explain whether Oct. 1 is included or not and should be changed into:

This contract will come into effect from and including October 1, 2015.

(3) This product is absolutely the best one on the market.

This is the overstatement of the fact, and the sentence should be changed into:

This product is the best one we can supply.

(4) We assure you that this error will never occur.

Similarly this sentence can be changed into the following:

We will do all we can so that we may not repeat such an error.

1.2 The Style and Tone of Business Letter Writing

1.2.1 Conversational Style

A good letter should reflect the personality of the writer and needs to be pleasing to the reader. In a good letter a conversation is held. People who write with a sense of personal contact have a better chance to make what they say interesting and convincing than those who feel they are writing letters.[7] Whatever you talk about in a letter, the language you use should be the same as if you met the person on the street, at home, or in the office. Such a language is warm and natural. It is also the language we use most and understand best.

But when faced with a writing task, many of us tend to change character. Instead of writing in friendly, conversational language, we write in stiff and stilted words. There is a misconception that big words and difficult words are preferred in business letters, but the result of such words is a cold and unnatural style — one that does not produce the goodwill effect you want your letters to have.

1.2.2 Avoid the Archaic Language of Business

Early English business writers borrowed heavily from the formal language of law and from the flowery language of the nobility.[8] From these two sources they developed a style of letter writing that became known as the "language of business". It was a cold, stiff, and unnatural style, but it was generally accepted throughout the English-speaking world, for instance, "wherein you state as per your letter", "take the liberty of", "acknowledge receipt of", etc.

Obviously the tone is cold, out of date, and a good writer should take care to give up such stale expressions.

1.2.3 Use Positive Language and Avoid Anger

People enjoy and react favorably to positive messages. A positive tone builds the reader's confidence in the writer's ability to solve problems and strengthens personal and business relationships. Positive words are usually best for letter goals, especially when persuasion and good will are needed. Positive words emphasize the pleasant aspects of the goal and tend to put the reader in the right frame of mind.[9] They also create the goodwill atmosphere readers seek in most letters.

When confronted with frustration, writer sometimes may lose temper and get angry, but rarely is anger justified in letters, because it destroys goodwill. Most of comments made in anger take many forms like sarcasm, insults and exclamation, and do not provide needed information.

The effect of angry words is to make the reader angry. With both writer and reader angry, the two are not likely to get together on whatever the letter is about. A tactful writer can refer courteously to the subject matter to avoid jeopardizing goodwill.[10] But when pleasant, positive words have not brought desired results, negative words may be justified.

1.3 Preparation before Writing

As a writer, you should make preparation for your creative works before taking up the pen. Generally speaking, the following should be borne in mind.

1.3.1 Studying Your Reader's Interest

It means that you should think of what your reader thinks.

To achieve this, you should "put yourself in your reader's shoes" and try to imagine how he will feel about what you write.[11] Ask yourself constantly, "What are his needs, his wishes, his interests, his problems to be solved, and how can I meet his requirements."

1.3.2 Planning What You Will Write and Writing Effectively

In order to plan what you write better and to write effectively, you should draft an outline before writing. Every language has its own features. For Chinese students, English is a foreign language. They had better learn to think and write directly in English and draft an English outline before writing.

1.3.3 Deciding to Adopt the Proper Layout, Tone and Style

As we can see, there are many kinds of practical English writing. Different kinds of practical English writing have different layouts, which will be discussed in the next unit. As a good letter writer, he or she should know well about how to adopt an appropriate layout.

1.4 Writing Naturally and Sincerely

Writing naturally and sincerely is to reveal your true feelings between lines, make sure that what you write would sound sincere and natural and try to avoid the affected words and florid style with little content.[12] In addition, as a writer, he or she should also learn to use polite language and be considerate to your readers.

Words and Vocabulary

proficiency	n.	能力
courtesy	n.	礼貌，彬彬有礼
verify	v.	核实，证实
jargon	n.	行话，黑话
misleading	a.	让人产生误解的，产生歧义的
equivocal	a.	含糊的，模糊的，意义不明的
concise	a.	简洁的，扼要的
steamer	n.	海轮，货轮
register	v.	登记，注册
accountant	n.	会计
wordy	a.	多言的，冗长的
fancy	a.	装饰的，（文体）华丽的
compose	v.	写（信），谱曲，组成
pithy	a.	简练的，精辟的
herewith	ad.	至此，用此方法
consummate	a.	完美无缺的，完善的
terminate	v.	结束
remunerate	v.	报酬，酬劳
converse	v.	交谈，谈话

hereto	ad.	（正式用语）于此
lengthy	a.	冗长的，啰唆的
courteous	a.	有礼貌的
abbreviate	v.	简略为，缩减为
reveal	v.	显示，表明
visualize	v.	想象，使直观化
initiative	n.	主动
commanding	a.	命令的，盛气凌人的
imperative	a.	祈使句的，强制的
subjunctive	a.	虚拟的
catalogue	n.	产品目录
mitigation	n.	减轻，缓解
overemphasize	v.	过分强调
irritating	a.	让人恼怒的，使激怒的
accordingly	ad.	因此，因而
abstract	a.	抽象的
misinterpretation	n.	误解，误读
comprise	v.	包括，包含
commission	n.	佣金
stilted	a.	（指文体等）不自然的，生硬的
misconception	n.	错误的认识，错误的观念
archaic	a.	过时的，陈旧的
flowery	a.	（文体）华丽的，辞藻华丽的
nobility	n.	高雅，高贵
stale	a.	陈旧的，陈腐的
sarcasm	n.	讽刺，讥讽
exclamation	n.	感叹，惊叹
tactful	ad.	策略的，讲究策略的
jeopardize	v.	破坏，危害
layout	n.	结构，布局
appropriate	a.	合适的，恰当的
affected	a.	不自然的，做作的
florid	a.	华丽的

Notes

1. See to it that all the matters are stated or discussed, and all the questions are answered or explained. 确保所有的事项都已陈述或讨论过，以及所有的问题都已回答或解释过。
本句中的"see to it that"为"确认，确定"的意思。

2. Basically, the writer should keep off anything that might be misleading or avoid using the words, and sentences that are equivocal in meaning. 从根本上来说，作者应该避免一切引起误解的内容，或者应避免使用一些含糊不清的文字。

3. The idea of keeping related words together — and as close together as possible — is probably the "whole idea" behind studying modifiers. 将相关的词尽可能近地写在一起也许是学习修饰语写作的一个根本原则。

4. Review of actual business correspondence reveals that special attention should be devoted to assuming the courtesy of business communication. 对现有商务信函的研究表明，人们尤其需要关注商务交流的礼貌性。

5. Effective writers visualize the reader before starting to write. 效率高的作者在动笔写信之前，应对读者进行一番想象。

6. Business writing should be vivid, specific and definite rather than vague, general and abstract, especially when the writer is requiring a response, solving problems, making an offer or acceptance, etc. 商务写作应立足生动、具体、明确，而不是含糊、泛泛而谈和抽象，尤其当作者需要对方做出回应，需要解决问题，发盘或接受发盘时。

7. People who write with a sense of personal contact have a better chance to make what they say interesting and convincing than those who feel they are writing letters. 如果作者将写信看作是与对方面对面的交流，他就比那些将写信仅仅看作是写信的人更能使其所写的一切有意思，且令人信服。
本句中的"with a sense of..."是"有……意识"的意思。

8. Early English business writers borrowed heavily from the formal language of law and from the flowery language of the nobility. 当初，一些商务英语信函的作者从正规的法律英语和贵族使用的华丽文辞中借鉴了大量的正式用语。

9. Positive words emphasize the pleasant aspects of the goal and tend to put the reader in the right frame of mind. 积极而正面的句子会渲染写作目的中令人愉快的方面，使读者保持一份好的心情。
本句中的"to put the reader in the right frame of mind"意为"使对方处于一个好的心情当中"。

10. A tactful writer can refer courteously to the subject matter to avoid jeopardizing goodwill. 讲究策略的作者会很礼貌地让对方留意信的"事由"，以避免伤害友谊。

11. To achieve this, you should "put yourself in your reader's shoes" and try to imagine how he

will feel about what you write. 为了实现这一点，你应该将自己放在读者的位置，并设想一下他在读信时的感受。

本句中的"put yourself in your reader's shoes"意为"设身处地替对方想一想"。

12. ... make sure that what you write would sound sincere and natural and try to avoid the affected words and florid style with little content. ……你应该保证你所写的一切必须真诚、自然，应避免使用矫揉造作、华而不实的句子。

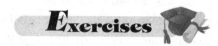

I Rewrite the following sentences to make them concise and clear.

1. We ask you to send your product catalogue for all kinds of goods being handled by your corporation for reference with your buyers.
2. We are famous computers importers and there are branches in three neighboring cities.
3. American business has a goal, which is to try to raise the standard of living.
4. It is true that often great affluence is accompanied by another problem, unrest socially.
5. Adam Smith as a matter of fact arrived at the conclusion that the division of labor makes it possible to increase the amount of goods we produce; this was in 1776.
6. In socialist economies as well as in capitalist economies, increasing numbers of workers who are highly qualified are unable to find job required by their skills and by their training.
7. The salesperson told us that we should write to the main office directly for whatever information we were in need of.
8. The convention, which was scheduled for the month of January was cancelled due to the fact that there are restriction placed on travel.
9. It goes without saying that we are acquainted with your policy on filing tax returns, and we have every intention of complying with the regulation, which you have stated.
10. In the event that you cannot accept our invitation to come to the meeting, we would appreciate your informing us of this fact as soon as possible.

II Revise the following sentences to make them positive rather than negative in tone.

1. Your misunderstanding of our February 9th letter caused you to make this mistake.
2. Unfortunately your shipment cannot be delivered until next week.
3. Your carelessness in this matter caused the damage to the computer system.
4. To avoid the damages to your image of company, please remit your payment within ten days.
5. We regret to inform you that we cannot accept the method of payment you suggested for this shipment.

6. You cannot visit our assembly line except on Saturday.
7. We have received your complaint about the late arrival of the consignment. We close at ... % p. m.
8. We do not believe that you will have cause for dissatisfaction.
9. Your order will be delayed for two weeks.

III Change the following wordy phrases into concise ones.

1. are desirous of
2. as a general rule
3. as per your suggestion
4. consider favorably
5. due in large measure to
6. in all probability
7. in the process of preparation
8. in the event that
9. in the normal course of
10. in view of the fact that
11. during the time of
12. enclosed herewith
13. for the reason that
14. fullest possible extent
15. give consideration to
16. make inquiry regarding
17. on the grounds that
18. not in a position to
19. pertaining to
20. pursuant to our agreement

IV Correct the mistakes in the following letter.

Dear Sirs,

We thank you for your letter of Oct. 12 regarded iron scraps, for which you have received inquiries from your customers in Africa.

We wish we had received your inquiry a little earlier. On the very day it reached us, a contract was placed with Mexico for a total of 360,000 tons. Because of this, our government has decided not to grant export licenses for the commodity for areas other than Mexico until December 31, 2015, expected the shortage, which may be caused in the domestic market.

Therefore, we shall be pleased to inform you with detail as soon as the circumstances becomes favor for us to do business in this line.

Yours sincerely

V Compare the following letters and tell which one is better and why.

Letter A

Dear Sirs,

We wish to acknowledge receipt of your credit application dated February 17 giving trade and bank references, and we thank you for the same. Please be advised that credit accommodations are herewith extended as per your request and your order has been shipped.

Hoping you will give us the opportunity of serving you again in the near future, we remain ready for it.

Very truly yours

Letter B

Dear Sirs,

Thank you for sending so promptly the trade and bank references we have asked for. I am glad to say that your order has already been shipped on the terms you requested.

We hope you will give us the chance to serve you again.

Very truly yours,

Unit 2

The Structure and Styles of Business Letters
商务信函的结构与格式

Although there are different ways in business writing, people usually follow a certain standardized way in their business communication. Generally speaking, a business letter should consist of the following seven principal parts:

(1) Letterhead;
(2) Date;
(3) Inside Name and Address;
(4) Salutation;
(5) Body of a Letter;
(6) Complimentary Close;
(7) Signature.

The above seven parts must be involved in your business letters. But depending on different purposes and options, a business letter will also present some other elements, such as:

(1) Reference No.;
(2) Attention Line;
(3) Subject/Caption;
(4) Enclosure;
(5) Carbon Copy;
(6) Postscript.

2.1 Principal Parts

2.1.1 Letterhead

Letterhead can also be called heading of the letter. It is usually placed on the top of a letter.

Besides the name and address, sometimes it also gives the relevant information about the sender's company, such as telephone number, fax number, internet address, email address, etc.

2.1.2 Date

The date is typed a few lines below the last line of the letterhead. In business letters, date line is very important. You can decide from the date line whether an order is fulfilled, a contract or an agreement is in effect, or a bill is paid.[1] Therefore, it should not be wrongly written or omitted.

Generally speaking, there are two ways in writing the date. You can write it in the logical order of day, month, year, for instance, 12th Dec., 2015. Or you can write the date after the month and use a comma between the day and the year, e.g. Dec. 22nd, 2015.

You had better use ordinal numbers for the day. And do not give the date figures as it may easily cause confusion. Different from the place in a Chinese letter, the date in an English letter should be put above the inside name and address.

2.1.3 Inside Address

The address of the organization receiving the letter is typed single-spaced at the left margin. This part usually refers to the recipient's name and address. The information should be given in a way like this:

(1) Receiver's name or his official title;
(2) Company's name;
(3) Number of the house and name of the street;
(4) District, name of the town or city;
(5) State or province, ZIP code;
(6) Name of country.

Here is an example:

> President
> Shanghai Foreign Trade & Economics Training Center
> 89, Fuzhou RD.
> Huangpu District, Shanghai, 200000
> P. R. C.

Sometimes Messrs., which is the plural form of Mr., is placed as a courtesy title before the name of a company which includes a personal element. For instance:

> Messrs. Evans & Sons Co. Ltd.

Unit 2 The Structure and Styles of Business Letters

2.1.4 Salutation

For most letter styles, place the letter greeting or salutation two lines below the last line of the inside address or the attention line (if used). If the letter is addressed to an individual, use that person's courtesy title and last name, e.g. Dear Miss Helen. The salutation varies according to the writer-recipient relations and the formality level of the letter.[2] "Dear Sir", "Dear Sir or Madam" or "Dear Sirs" and "Ladies and Gentlemen" can be used to address a person of whom you know neither the name nor the gender.

Sometimes some special titles may be used as the salutation. They are preceded by "Dear" and followed by the surname only, e.g.[3] Dear Dr. Watson, or Dear Prof. Young. Be sure to add a colon or a comma (not a semicolon) after the salutation.

Examples of typical salutations are:

> Dear Mr. ×××
> Dear Mrs. ×××
> Dear Miss. ×××
> Dear Ms. ×××
> Dear Dr. ×××
> Dear Prof. ×××
> Dear Sir(s)
> Gentlemen
> Ladies and Gentlemen
> To Whom It May Concern

2.1.5 Body of the Letter

This is the most important part of a letter in which you convey the real information. Before you write it, you must consider two points as follows:

(1) What is the purpose to write this letter?
(2) How to present the letter in the best way?

No matter whether your letter is long or short, it usually consists of three paragraphs: the opening paragraph which is to give a subject introduction of the letter; the middle paragraph to discuss the details of the transaction; and the closing paragraph to end the letter in a way of summation, further request or suggestion.[4] And when writing the letter, you should attach great importance to the 7 C's principles[5]: Clearness, Conciseness, Consideration, Courtesy, Correctness, Concreteness and Completeness.

2.1.6 Complimentary Close

The complimentary closeness is merely a polite way to bring the letter to an end. If the salutation is "Dear Sirs", "Dear Madam or Sir", you will use "Yours faithfully", "Faithfully yours" as complimentary close. If the salutation is "Gentlemen", "Mr./Mrs./Miss/Ms. White", etc., you can use: Yours sincerely, Sincerely yours, Yours truly, Truly yours. "Best wishes" or "Best regards" can also be used in less formal letters. It is often given from the second line below the closing sentence of the letter.

2.1.7 Signature

Signature is placed three blank lines below the complimentary close. It usually consists of three lines like this:

(1) Manual signature of the writer;
(2) Typed name of the writer and his or her job title.

2.2 Optional Elements

2.2.1 Attention Line

If you send your message officially to an organization, an attention line allows you to send it directly to a specific individual, officer, or department. However, if you know an individual's complete name, it is always better to use it as the first line of the inside address and avoid an attention line.

2.2.2 Subject Line

A subject line helps identify the subject of the letter. Although experts suggest placing the subject line two lines below the salutation, many businesses actually place it above the salutation. Use whatever style your organization prefers. Using a subject line will alert your reader to the content of your message and enable him or her to decide whether the letter requires immediate attention.[6] So a subject line is often underlined or typed in capitals.

2.2.3 Enclosure

If an enclosure or attachment accompanies the letter, a notation to that effect should be placed four or five lines below the signature.[7] The word "enclosure" or shortened "enc." or "encl." followed by a period or colon should be written. For example:

    Enc. Bill of Lading (6 copies)
       Commercial invoice (4 copies)
       Insurance policy

2.2.4 Copy Notation

If copies of a business letter have been made for other individuals, a copy notation is typed one or two lines below the enclosure notation (if used). A colon following is optional. Most people prefer to use notation like CC, cc, Cc, (all mean carbon copy). Since most copies are now photocopied, some people use the notation XC (Xerox copy), PC (photo copy), or C (copy). However, if you do not want the addressee to know that someone else is receiving a copy, do not include this notation on the original copy.

2.2.5 Postscript

A postscript (P.S.) is an afterthought, and it is usually a sign of poor planning in formal letter.[8] But as a special device, it has two legitimate functions.

(1) Some executives occasionally add a postscript to add a personal touch to the typewritten letter.
(2) Writers of sales letter often withhold one last convincing argument for emphatic inclusion in a postscript, e.g. P.S. ... to see you at the annual sales meeting on October 16.

2.3 Styles of a Business Letter

There are several acceptable styles for business letter. The four most popular forms are indented style, full block style, semi-block style and modified block style.

2.3.1 Indented Style

The main feature in this style is that each line of the inside name and address should be indented 2-3 spaces, and the first line of each paragraph should be indented 3-8 spaces.

Letter Head

                                                          Date

Inside Address
□□_____
   □□_____
      □□_____

Salutation

                                   Body

□□□□_____
_____

□□□□_____
_____

                                          Complimentary Close

                                          Signature
                                          _____
                                          _____

2.3.2 Semi-block Style

    It's a combination of indented style and modified block style. It is very similar to the indented style with the only difference that the inside address should start neatly from the left-hand side of the sheet. Please look at the following simplified format.

Unit 2 The Structure and Styles of Business Letters

Letter Head

Date

Inside Address

Salutation

Body

Complimentary Close

Signature

2.3.3 | Modified Block Style

According to this style, the first line of each paragraph in the letter body is not indented, while the letterhead, date line, complimentary close, and signature are aligned slightly past the center of the sheet. Let us look at the simplified format.

2.3.4 Full Block Style

Letterhead is laid out in the center of the letter, while the rest elements of a business letter start from the left-hand side of the sheet neatly. Open punctuation is adopted for the inside address, which means that both sender's address and recipients' address must avoid using more punctuations.

The body of the letter has double spacing between the paragraphs. Typists generally prefer the full block format, for it has a simple appearance, and is quicker to type. The following is the indication of this style.

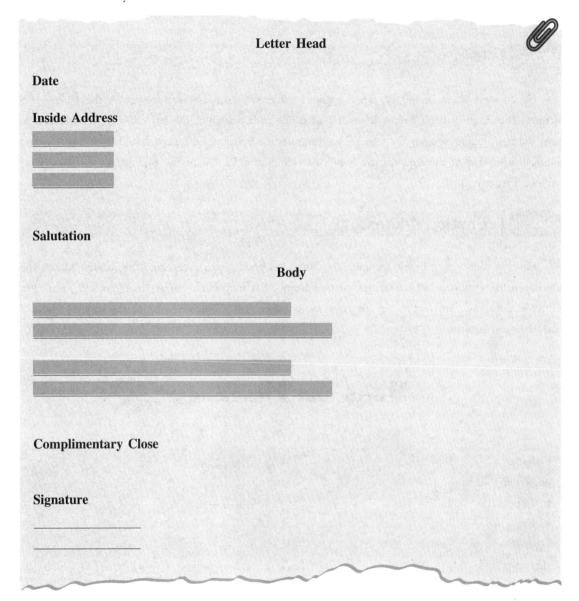

2.4 Spacing, Margin and Envelop Addressing

2.4.1 Spacing

Most business letters are single-spaced with the exception of extremely short and one-paragraphed letters, which are usually typed with double spaces between lines. However, there should always be a double space line between paragraphs. As for the spacing between such parts as the date line and the letterhead, the signature and the complimentary close, they are described respectively in the layout of a business letter.

2.4.2 Margin

No business letters should be typed without margins, which are as necessary as the frames of a picture. The simplest method is to leave at least a one-inch margin at the left side of the letter and to keep the right margin roughly the same. The margin at the bottom of the page should be at least one and one-half times that of the side margins while the same is applicable to the top margin of plain paper without a letterhead.

2.4.3 Envelop Addressing

Envelop addressing calls for accuracy, legibility and good appearance. Like the inside address, the address on the envelope can be written in two forms: the indented form and the blocked form. No matter in which way the address on the envelope is written, it should conform to the inside address in both style and content.

Words and Vocabulary

salutation	n.	致敬，问候
enclosure	n.	附件
postscript	n.	（信末等签名后的）附笔，附言
recipient	n.	收信人
gender	n.	性别
precede	v.	在……之前
complimentary	a.	致意的，问候的
manual	a.	手工的
identify	v.	确认，辨认
alert	v.	使警觉
capital	n.	大写字母
notation	n.	标注，注明
addressee	n.	被称呼人，收信人
legitimate	a.	合法的
touch	n.	色彩

Unit 2 The Structure and Styles of Business Letters

withhold	v.	抵挡住，制止，阻止
indented	a.	缩行式的
align	v.	使……成一直线
punctuation	n.	标点
indication	n.	表明，注明
respectively	ad.	各自地，分别地
legibility	n.	容易辨认
complimentary close		客套结束语
reference No.		编号
attention line		指定收信人姓名
carbon copy		抄送
ordinal number		序号
bill of lading		提单
commercial invoice		商业发票
insurance policy		保险单
indented style		缩行式
full block		齐头式
semi-block		半齐头式
modified block		改良齐头式

Notes

1. You can decide from the date line whether an order is fulfilled, a contract or an agreement is in effect, or a bill is paid.　从信的日期中你便能了解到订单是否已执行，合同或协议是否仍然有效，货款是否已经支付。
   本句中的"bill"为"货款"的意思。

2. The salutation varies according to the writer-recipient relations and the formality level of the letter.
   称呼的变化取决于作者与读者之间的关系及信的正式程度。

3. Sometimes some special titles may be used as the salutation. They are preceded by "Dear" and followed by the surname only, e.g. …　有时在称呼前加一些特殊的头衔，并在这些特殊的头衔前再加上"Dear"，然后在头衔后仅仅加上姓氏，例如……

4. … and the closing paragraph to end the letter in a way of summation, further request or suggestion.
   ……以总结的形式来完成信的结尾，并进一步提出请求和建议。

5. And when writing the letter, you should attach great importance to the 7 C's principles … 写信时，你应该重视"7C 原则"……
   本句中的"attach great importance to"意为"重视，强调"。

6. Using a subject line will alert your reader to the content of your message and enable him or her to decide whether the letter requires immediate attention. 在信中注明"事由"可以使读者留意信的内容,从而决定该信是否需要读一下。

7. If an enclosure or attachment accompanies the letter, a notation to that effect should be placed four or five lines below the signature. 附件注明,或者类似这样的注明应该置于署名位置以下四至五行的地方。

8. A postscript (P.S.) is an afterthought, and it is usually a sign of poor planning in formal letter. 附笔标注(可缩写为P.S.或PS)用以补充信写完后又想说的话,它在正式的信函中通常是一种考虑欠缺的表现。

Exercises

I Arrange the following information in a proper form as they should be set out in a business letter.

1. Sender's name: China National Textiles Import & Export Corporation, Shanghai Branch
2. Sender's address: 18th Floor, Sunshine Mansion, 567 Siping Rd., Hongkou District, Shanghai, 200000, P.R.C.
3. Sender's fax number: 86-21-63209767
4. Sender's e-mail address: shanghaitextiles@shtextiles.com.cn
5. Date: March 2nd, 2015
6. Receiver's name: W.G. Wilkinson Co., Ltd.
7. Receiver's address: 789 Maple Street, Lagos, Nigeria
8. Salutation: Dear Sirs
9. Subject: embroidered table-cloths
10. The Message: We thank you for your letter of Feb. 24th inquiring for the captioned goods. The enclosed booklet contains details of all our embroidered table-cloths and will enable you to make a suitable selection. We look forward to receiving your specific enquiry with keen interest.
11. Complimentary close: Yours faithfully

II Read the following letter and try to point out the problems in this letter.

DATATECH
International, Inc. 4038 Candlewood Drive
Lakewood, California 90711 Tel (213) 92659023
2015/7/6

Unit 2 The Structure and Styles of Business Letters

Clara J. Smith
Office Occupations Department
North Seattle Co., Ltd.
9600 College Way North
Seattle, WA 98103 -3599

Dear Sirs,

Ref: Request for urgent shipment

Attention: Office Occupation Department

We enclose our figures of sales in your product during the past three months. You will see that our sales of the special line are quite disappointing. We requested your urgent shipment of this product, which you accepted. However, five weeks went by before the goods arrived instead of three weeks and we lost a wonderful opportunity of sales.

When inquiring about this matter we found that the goods were not shipped until four weeks after the date of dispatch. If they had been delivered straight to Qingdao, much valuable time would have been saved. It will be necessary for you to give us your very best attention if you wish to maintain a certain level of sales in this market.

Best wishes

Yours faithfully

Elizabeth R. St. James,
Manager, Customer Relations Dept.

III Fill in each of the blanks in the following letter with an appropriate word or expressions given in the box.

but, comparable, attention, to, set, appreciate, dependable, fresh

Dear Mr. Smith,

Your recent experience with a _____ of Monday flashlight batteries is given proper _____. Under separate cover, please find a new flashlight of _____ value with the one you submitted us under guarantee. Fresh Monday batteries are included.

For more than 99.5 percent of our entire Monday battery production is satisfying. It would be nice if this record was 100 percent, _____ in the absence of a perfect record, we do _____ it when a customer brings an unsatisfactory experience to our attention.

We are sure that the _____ Monday batteries we are sending you will give you the same _____ service that has made Monday batteries so famous all over the world.

Very truly yours,

IV Writing practice.

Write a business letter to one of your friends in the format you prefer, in which you give a brief account of ways to keep your letter a neat appearance.

Unit 3

Establishing Business Relations
与对方建立商务关系

3.1 Introduction

Establishing business relations with prospective dealers is one of the important measures to maintain or expand business activities in doing foreign trade.[1] Customers are the basis of business expansion, therefore, it is a common practice in business communications that newly established firms or firms that wish to enlarge their business scope and turnover write letters to new customers for the establishment of relations.[2]

One can obtain such desired information as names and addresses of the firms to be dealt with through advertisements, trade directories, trade negotiations, banks, chambers of commerce both at home and abroad, commercial counselor's offices, trade presses, exhibitions and trade fairs, market surveys, inquiries received from foreign merchants, branch offices or representatives abroad, introduction of connections, business houses of the same trade and the Internet.

When having obtained the desired name and address of the firm from any of the above sources, one can write a letter or a circular to the other party. Generally speaking, this kind of letter includes the following ones.

(1) The source of the information, i. e., how and where the writer gets the name and address of the receiver's company.
(2) The intention or desire of writing the letter.
(3) Self-introduction, including the business scope, branches and other necessary information.
(4) The references as to the financial status and integrity of the writer's company.
(5) Expectation of cooperation and an early reply.

Traders must do everything possible to consolidate their established relations with the existing customers and also develop and revitalize the trade by searching for new connections.[3] If they are to buy some products, they may ask for samples, price lists, catalogues or other reference materials. The letters should be written politely, clearly and concisely. As regards the receiver of such kind of letter, he or she is recommended to answer in full without any delay to create goodwill, leaving a positive impression on the other party and possibly expand the trade between each other.[4]

3.2　Letter Samples

 Letter 3-1（A letter written by an exporter to an importer）

Dear Sirs,

We come to know through the Commercial Counselor's Office of the Chinese Embassy in Morocco the name and address of your firm.[5] We also learn from them that you are in the market for textiles.

Our company specializes in exporting textile products to various foreign countries. We wish to enter into business relations with you by the commencement of some practical transactions.[6]

To give you a general idea of the various kinds of textile products now available for export, we are enclosing here our latest brochure and a price list for your reference. We shall be pleased to give you our lowest quotation upon receipt of your detailed requirements.

We look forward to receiving from you soon.

Yours faithfully,

Joel Mandelstam

 Letter 3-2（A letter written by an importer to a producer）

Dear Sirs,

We owe your name and address to Showner Co., Ltd., Paris, through which we understand[7] that you are interested in establishing business relations with Chinese companies for selling cosmetic products of your country.

We have been importers of cosmetic products for many years. We should appreciate the catalogues and quotations of your products, and we shall gladly study the sales possibilities in our market.

We hope you will give us an early reply.

Yours faithfully,

Alfred Liu

📧 **Letter 3-3** (**A letter written by a tea producer to an importer**)

Dear Sirs,

From the Chamber of Commerce of Beijing, we have come to know the name of your firm and take the pleasure of addressing this letter to you in the hope of establishing business relations with you.

We specialize in the exportation of various tea products, which have enjoyed great popularity in the world market. We enclose our latest catalogue for your inspection and hope that you would contact us if any item is of interest to you.

We are looking forward to your favorable and prompt reply.

Yours faithfully,

Lucia Tan

📧 **Letter 3-4** (**A letter written by an import and export company to another**)

Dear Sirs,

You were kindly recommended to us by the Chamber of Commerce of Stockholm. We shall be pleased to enter into direct business relations with you.

Our company is one of the greatest import and export companies in China and has wide experience in all the lines we handle.[8] We mainly export such items as electronics and electrical appliances, light industrial products and chemicals. Our imported goods include information technology products, luxurious automobiles and cosmetic products.

China is a very big market with increasing purchasing power. We would like to establish a business relation between us and to be an exclusive agent for your company in China. If you want to import some materials or products from China, we can supply all our help.

Our banker is the Bank of China, Stockholm branch, and it can provide you with detailed information about our business and finances.
We are looking forward to a productive trade between us.

Yours faithfully,

Charlie Qi
Manager

Letter 3-5 (A letter written by a producer to a commercial counselor's office)

Dear Sirs,

We thank you for your cooperation for our business.

We want to enlarge our trade in porcelain teacups and saucers, but unfortunately we have no good connections in Luxemburg. Therefore, we shall be obliged if you introduce us to the most capable and reliable importers in that country who are possibly interested in our products.

Your information on this respect will be highly appreciated.

Yours faithfully,

Arthur Xie

Unit 3 Establishing Business Relations

 Letter 3-6（A letter written by a bag producer to an importer）

Dear Sirs,

We learned from your advertisement in the May 8th issue of China Daily that you are dealing in bags.

We sell bags made of various materials. They are of good quality and have fine workmanship. Besides, the designs are quite attractive. Chinese bags are very popular in many European countries with their lower prices and superior quality.⁹ We would like to work with you to market them in France.

We send you separately by airmail a copy of the latest catalog.¹⁰ Please let us know if there are any items which are of interest to you, and we will send you our quotations and samples.

We look forward to your early reply.

Yours faithfully,

Zhang Changsheng
Manager

 Letter 3-7（A letter written by an importer to a software producer）

Dear Sirs,

The Bank of China here has recommended your corporation as being interested in establishing business relations with China corporations for selling softwares of your country.

We are one of the principal importers of softwares in China and are interested in importing softwares on accounting and management. We invite you to send us details and prices of your products, and shall be glad to study the sales possibilities at our end.

We shall always be happy to hear from you and will carefully consider any proposals likely to lead to business between us.

Yours faithfully,

Arthur Doyle

Letter 3-8 (A letter written by a porcelain producer to an importer)

Dear Sirs,

We get to know your corporation from our office in Beijing that you are one of the largest importers of porcelain products in your country. We would like to take this opportunity to approach you for the establishment of trade relations with you.[11]

We specialize in producing various porcelain products, and our goods have been accepted by domestic and overseas clients for over hundreds of years, enjoying a good popularity. Should you favor us with inquiries for your specific requirements, we could supply you with first-class goods at competitive prices.

It is our hope to promote, by joint efforts, both trade and friendship to our mutual advantage. We look forward to receiving from you good news.

Yours faithfully,

Kathy Yi

Letter 3-9 (A letter to a bank asking for information)

Dear Sirs,

We have recently received a letter from Gloryshield Company in Sweden. The company introduced itself to us as one of the leading importers and wholesalers of electronic products in South Africa, and hopes to establish business relations with us and promote the sales of our products in Germany. The following is the address of the Gloryshield Company shown on the envelope of the letter sent to us:

Gloryshield Electronic Equipment Trading Co., Ltd.
Hammets Crossing Office Park Block 126/9 23
Selbourne Avenue Fourways Sandton 3168
South Africa

We should be obliged if you would provide us with the necessary information about the company. Any information you may obtain for us will be treated as strictly confidential.

Yours faithfully,

Perry Wang

Words and Vocabulary

prospective	a.	将来的，未来的
dealer	n.	经销商，商人
expand	v.	发展，扩张
practice	n.	实践，操作
advertisement	n.	广告
exhibition	n.	展览
inquiry	n.	询盘
merchant	n.	商人
representative	n.	代表处
connection	n.	联系，关系
circular	n.	通知，通函，广告
source	n.	来源
reference	n.	参考，参照
integrity	n.	完整，完全，完整性
expectation	n.	期待，预料
trader	n.	商人
consolidate	v.	巩固，加强
revitalize	v.	使恢复元气，使有新的活力
concisely	ad.	简洁地
recommend	v.	推荐，建议
embassy	n.	大使馆
goodwill	n.	善意，亲切，商誉
Morocco	n.	摩洛哥
commencement	n.	开始，发端

transaction	n.	交易
brochure	n.	小册子
cosmetic	n.	化妆品
quotation	n.	报价单,行情表
popularity	n.	普及,流行,声望
favorable	a.	赞成的,有利的,赞许的
prompt	a.	迅速的,即时的
Stockholm	n.	斯德哥尔摩(瑞典首都)
line	n.	行业,领域
electronic	a.	电子的
luxurious	a.	奢侈的,奢华的
Luxemburg	n.	卢森堡
reliable	a.	可靠的
workmanship	n.	工艺,做工
software	n.	软件
accounting	n.	会计
proposal	n.	建议,方案
Netherlands	n.	荷兰
approach	v.	接近,动手处理
specialize	v.	从事,经营
favor	n.	支持,赞成,照顾
confidential	a.	保密的,秘密的

business scope	经营范围
trade directory	贸易黄页,贸易电话簿
trade negotiation	贸易谈判
chamber of commerce	商会
trade press	贸易新闻,贸易简报
trade fair	商品交易会
market survey	市场调查
branch office	分公司
business house	商行,商店
financial status	财政状况
existing customers	现有顾客
price list	价格单
commercial counselor's office	商务处
textile products	纺织产品
electrical appliances	家用电器

Unit 3 Establishing Business Relations

light industrial products	轻工产品
information technology products	信息技术产品，IT 产品
exclusive agent	独家代理
porcelain cups and saucers	陶瓷杯碟
sales possibilities	销售可能性
joint efforts	合作，共同努力

Notes

1. Establishing business relations with prospective dealers is one of the important measures to maintain or expand business activities in doing foreign trade. 在对外贸易中，同潜在客户建立商务关系是维持或拓展业务的重要措施之一。

    本句中的"prospective"意思是"潜在的，有希望的"，"maintain"意为"维持，保持"。

2. ... it is a common practice in business communications that newly established firms or firms that wish to enlarge their business scope and turnover write letters to new customers for the establishment of relations. ……在商务沟通中，常见的做法是新建公司或希望扩大经营范围和业务量的公司写信给新客户，以求建立贸易关系。

    本句中的"common practice"意为"常见的做法或实践"，"newly established firms"的意思是"新建或新成立的公司"。

3. Traders must do everything possible to consolidate their established relations with the existing customers and also develop and revitalize the trade by searching for new connections. 贸易商必须尽最大可能巩固同现有客户已建立的贸易关系，同时还要寻找新的客户关系来发展和扩大贸易。

    本句中的"existing"意为"现有的，当前的"。

4. As regards the receiver of such kind of letter, he or she is recommended to answer in full without any delay to create goodwill, leave a positive impression on the other party and possibly expand the trade between each other. 作为收信一方，则应及时详细地回复，表达良好的意愿，给对方一个积极的印象，尽可能扩大彼此之间的贸易。

    本句中的"answer in full"意思是"充分或详细地回复"，"leave a positive impression on sb."意为"给某人留下积极的印象"。

5. We come to know through the Commercial Counselor's Office of the Chinese Embassy in Morocco the name and address of your firm. 承蒙中国驻摩洛哥大使馆商务处的帮助，我们得以知晓贵公司的名称和地址。

6. We wish to enter into business relations with you by the commencement of some practical transactions. 我们希望同贵方进行实际的交易，以建立贸易关系。

    本句中的"to enter into business relation with..."意为"和……建立贸易关系"。

7. We owe your name and address to Showner Co., Ltd., Paris, through whom we understand ... 经由巴黎秀奈尔有限责任公司的介绍，我们得知贵方公司的名称和地址，并了解到……

8. ... has wide experience in all the lines we handle. ……在我们从事的所有领域拥有广泛的经验。

9. Chinese bags are very popular in many European countries with their lower prices and superior quality. 中国包因其价格低廉，质量上乘，在许多欧洲国家都很受欢迎。

10. We send you separately by airmail a copy of the latest catalog. 我们将另函航空邮寄给贵方我们最新的产品目录。

11. We would like to take this opportunity to approach you for the establishment of trade relations with you. 我们希望借此机会同贵方建立贸易关系。
    本句中的"take this opportunity"是"利用这次机会"的意思。

Sentence Menu

1. Opening

(1) Through ..., we learn that you are interested in ...

(2) We owe your name and address to ... through which we learn that you were seeking partners in China for selling your ... products.

(3) Your company has been introduced to us by ... as prospective buyers of ... goods. As we handle these goods, we shall be pleased to enter into direct business relations with you.

(4) Your firm has been kindly recommended to us by ... as a large importer of furniture.

(5) On the recommendation of ..., we have learned with pleasure the name of your firm.

(6) We understood after contacting your trade delegation that you are one of the leading importers of ... goods in your area and wish to enter into business relations with us.

(7) We have been put in touch with you by your embassy here.

2. Introducing one's own company or line of product

(1) We would like to introduce ourselves to you with the hope that we may have a good chance of cooperation with you in your business extension.

(2) We would like to establish business relations with you.

(3) We have been in the line of ... for many years.

(4) Our competitive prices, superior quality and efficiency have won confidence and goodwill among our business clients.

(5) With reference to your letter of ... addressed to ... we are glad to inform you that it has been duly forwarded to us for attention and reply.

(6) Our market survey informs us that you have a keen interest in the import of . . .

(7) Specializing in the export of . . . , we wish to express our desire to trade with you in this line.

(8) We would like to write to you to enter into business relations with you.

(9) Your letter expressing the hope of establishing business connections with us has been received with thanks.

(10) We are writing to you in the hope that we can open up business relations with your firm.

3. Asking for information and ending

(1) Please let us know by return what your experience has been in your dealings with them.

(2) The above information is given confidentially and without responsibility on our part.

(3) Our mutual understanding and cooperation will certainly result in considerable business between us.

(4) It is hoped that by our joint efforts we can promote business as well as friendship.

(5) We shall be grateful if you will reply at an early date.

I Put the following terms or phrases from English into Chinese or vice versa.

1. workmanship
2. catalogue
3. consular
4. price list
5. specialize in
6. push the sales of
7. 另封邮寄
8. 开始（某种关系）
9. 按照他们的要求
10. 为了打开中国市场
11. 稳定的财政状况
12. 享有极佳的声誉

II Fill in the blanks of the following letters with the words given below, and change the form when necessary.

> inform, establish, reputation, proposal, specialize, opportunity, purpose, interest, owe

Dear Sirs,

We _____ your name and address to L&R Company, who has _____ us that you are _____ in entering the market in China. We hope to _____ business relations with you for the _____ of marketing your products here.

We like to take this _____ to introduce ourselves as one of the leading company in China mainly _____ in electronic products, with high _____ and reliable outlets.

To give you a general idea of our company, we are sending you separately a copy of our brochure. Any _____ concerning cooperation will be given our immediate consideration.

We are looking forward to your early reply.

Yours faithfully,

III Complete the following sentences with the Chinese given in the brackets.

1. We _____ (愿与贵公司建立贸易关系) on the basis of equality and mutual benefit.
2. It will be highly appreciated if you _____ (立即着手此事).
3. If your price is reasonable, we trust we can _____ (长期大量订货).
4. Our products are _____ (以质量上乘、工艺精湛而闻名), and have enjoyed great popularity both _____ (在国内外).
5. We _____ (借此机会) to introduce ourselves as a stated-owned corporation _____ (专营电子设备).
6. We would like to write to you and see if we can establish business relations _____ (通过开始几宗实际的交易).
7. _____ (承蒙驻贵国的中华人民共和国大使馆商务处告知贵方公司的名称和地址) who informed us that your are in the market for men's apparel.
8. _____ (兹介绍本公司为中国最大的丝绸出口商之一), having relations with more than 100 countries and regions in the world.
9. We are _____ (同这里的所有经销商关系密切), and feel sure we can sell large quantities of your goods if we get your offers at competitive prices.

IV Translate the following letter into English.

敬启者：

　　承蒙我国驻巴黎商务参赞处告知贵公司商号和地址，我们得知贵公司有意在中国开展业务。

　　今借此机会特向贵公司介绍，本公司多年来一直经营通讯设备，是中国主要经销商之一。如能收到你方产品目录和报价，将不胜感激，同时我方很愿意研究贵公司产品在我方市场的销售前景。

　　盼早日回复。

敬上

Unit 3 Establishing Business Relations

V **Writing practice.**

Situational Writing

Write a letter with the following hints.

- 经北京商会介绍，我方得知贵公司的名称和地址。
- 我公司专门经营电机产品出口业务。
- 我方另函寄去一本目录册。
- 如对目录中产品感兴趣，请询价。

Unit 4

Inquiries
询　购

4.1 Introduction

　　Inquiries are made when a businessperson intends to purchase certain goods or obtain desired services. The buyer usually sends an inquiry to invite a quotation or an offer from the seller, therefore inquiries mean potential business for both the buyer and the seller.

　　Based on the inquired contents, inquiries can be divided into general inquiries and specific inquiries. The writer of a general inquiry asks for general information, a catalogue, a price list, or a sample book, while that of a specific inquiry focuses on the detailed information about the specific target goods or services.[1]

　　Inquiries can also be classified into first inquiries and inquiries for repeat orders by the relationship between the writer and the recipient. A first inquiry is employed when the letter is sent to a seller with whom the buyer has not previously done business, and inquiries for repeat orders are mostly for acquainted customers. As for the latter one, the inquiry may be very simple and most often a printed inquiry form will be enough. Our focus of this unit will be on the writing of a first inquiry. In a first inquiry, it is useful for the writer to tell the recipient some information about his or her own business, the kinds of goods he or she needs, and the reasons for the inquiry to win trust from the other party. Besides, the writer needs to mention how he or she obtained the seller's name and address, the market analysis of the demand for the seller's goods or services, and the materials and information that he or she wants to receive. Mostly, the writer has interest in a catalogue, a price list, the seller's discounting policy, method of payment, delivery time and samples.[2] The following tips are of great value in guiding the preparation of letters of inquiries.

　　(1) State concisely and exactly the request.
　　(2) Enumerate the questions when there are many.
　　(3) Make a request for reply and let the seller feel the value of the information to you.
　　(4) Show courteousness and politeness.
　　(5) Give the seller some hope of substantial order or continued business.

4.2 Letter Samples

✉ **Letter 4-1**（An inquiry for nickel plated domestic products）

Dear Sirs,

Subject: Nickel-plated products

We should like you to send us a catalogue and price list regarding your nickel-plated domestic products.³ You were recommended to us by our colleagues at Amazon Industries in Los Angels with whom you have done business for a number of years.

This company produces a large range of domestic and office furniture, and we are interested in using a number of products from your current range in the manufacture of our goods. As we are about to expand our export operation, it is essential that our suppliers be both competitive in terms of price, and extremely reliable.

We will be interested in discussing terms with you as and when the final decision has been taken, but, prior to this, can you tell me what discounts you offer on bulk purchases?⁴

We look forward to hearing from you soon.

Yours faithfully,

Abraham Rice
General Manager

 Letter 4-2（An inquiry written to a textile company）

Dear Sir or Madam,

We are a company that imports carpets for sales to European clients and we have enclosed our company's brochure for your reference.

Your company's name is made to our attention through an article in the November issue of Textile Magazine and we understand that you manufacture carpets of various sizes. Since we are interested in doing business with your company, we should like to have some information about your company and your products. We would therefore appreciate your sending us your company's catalogue so that we can examine the business potential.

Yours faithfully,

Anna

Letter 4-3 (An inquiry for handbags)

Dear Sirs,

We have learned from one Australian company of the same trade that you are a dealer of handbags in a variety of leathers. We are interested in them, for there is a steady demand in our market for handbags of good quality.

We will be appreciative if you send us a copy of your handbag catalogue, with details of your price and terms of payment. It is helpful if you could also supply samples of the various leathers from which your handbags are made.

In view of the demand for your products[5], an immediate reply is appreciated.

Yours faithfully,

Tracy

Letter 4-4 (An inquiry for toolkits)

Dear Mr. Tony,

We are glad to learn from your letter of November 13 that as exporters of Chinese hardware goods, you intend to establish direct business connections with us.

We are interested in Harmon toolkit and please let us have your latest prices CFR together with your terms of payment and state your earliest delivery date and discounts for regular purchases.⁶

In order to acquaint us with the materials and workmanship of your products, we shall be pleased if you could send us your catalogues, sample books and other necessary information on Harmon toolkit.

Should your price be found competitive and terms acceptable, we intend to place a substantial order.

We look forward to your early reply.

Yours sincerely,

Lucy

Letter 4-5 (An inquiry for textile products)

Dear Mr. Li,

Subject: importers of garments

We purchased from you textile products last year and your products have been very satisfactory.

At present, we need a large quantity of garments as per the enclosed list. Please send us your pro forma invoice by fax and hard copy in quadruplicate by airmail. You are kindly requested to quote the CIF Los Angels rate.⁷

Owing to the fierce competition, it is important that your quotation would reach us not later than the end of this month so as not to miss the business chance.⁸

Your immediate attention to the above is appreciated.

Sincerely yours,

Gorge Rice
Manager

Encl.: inquiry list

 Letter 4-6（An inquiry for cotton blankets and bed sheets）

Dear Sirs,

We have been informed of your company and address through the Chamber of Commerce in Beijing. We are interested in your cotton blankets and bed-sheets for sales in the US and Canadian market.

We would like you to send us details of your various ranges, including sizes, colors, prices and samples of the different qualities of material used. We trust that you will make an effort to quote us most favorable terms for large quantities.

Looking forward to establishing direct business relations with you.

Yours faithfully,

Adam Smith
Manager

 Letter 4-7（An inquiry for sportswear）

Dear Sirs,

You are recommended to us by Bank of China in New York that you are one of the leading sportswear dealers. Right now, we are particularly interested in importing various ranges of sportswear.

It would be helpful if you could send us your latest catalogue and price list. If the quality of the goods comes up to our expectation and the delivery date is acceptable, we can probably let you have regular orders.

We are large dealers in textiles here and believe there is a promising market in our area for moderately priced ladies' and men's sportswear.

We are looking forward to your earliest reply.

Yours faithfully,

Paul Maidment
Manager

Letter 4-8 (An inquiry for digital cameras)

Dear Sirs,

We saw your digital cameras at the China Trade Fair in Guangzhou in October. The digital cameras you showed would be most suitable for our market. We are leading dealers of electronic products in Beijing and interested in purchasing your cameras. Would you please send us details of your cameras including the functions?

When you quote, please state terms of payment and discount you would allow on purchases of quantities not less than 1,000 sets. If your digital cameras are of good quality and the prices are in line, we will place regular large orders with you.

We should appreciate it greatly if you would give us a prompt reply.

Yours faithfully,

Zhao Tongbin
Manager

Words and Vocabulary

quotation	n.	价格，报价单
offer	n.	报价，出价，提议
inquiry	n.	询盘
catalogue	n.	目录
enumerate	v.	列举，列出
courteousness	n.	礼貌，礼节
appreciative	a.	表示感激的，承认有价值的
toolkit	n.	工具箱
quadruplicate	n.	一式四份的文件
general inquiry		一般询盘
specific inquiry		具体询盘
price list		价格目录，报价单
sample book		样品册
first inquiry		首次询盘
(the) method of payment		支付方式
delivery time		交货时间
substantial order		大额订单
nickel plated		镀镍
bulk purchase		大宗购买
CFR (Cost and Freight)		成本加运费
pro forma invoice		形式发票
CIF (Cost, Insurance and Freight)		成本保险加运费
fierce competition		竞争激烈
chamber of commerce		商会
digital camera		数码相机

Notes

1. The writer of a general inquiry asks for general information, a catalogue, a price list, or a sample book, while that of a specific inquiry focuses on the detailed information about the specific target goods or services. 一般询盘的内容包括常规信息、商品目录、价格目录或是样品册，

而具体询盘则重点了解目标商品或服务的具体信息。

本句中的"that"指代"the writer"。

2. Mostly, the writer has interest in a catalogue, a price list, the seller's discounting policy, the method of payment, delivery time and samples. 在大多数情况下，询盘人比较感兴趣的是产品目录、价格目录、卖方的折扣政策、支付方式、交货时间和样品。

3. We should like you to send us a catalogue and price list regarding your nickel-plated domestic products. 请将你们镀镍产品的目录和报价单寄给我们。

本句中的"regarding"意为"相关的，有关的"。

4. ... can you tell me what discounts you offer on bulk purchases? ……能否告知贵方大额订单的折扣政策？

本句中的"bulk"意思是"大额的，大宗的"。

5. In view of the demand for your products ... 鉴于市场对贵方产品的需求……

6. We are interested in Harmon toolkit and please let us have your latest prices CFR together with your terms of payment and state your earliest delivery date and discounts for regular purchases. 我们对哈门工具箱很感兴趣，请将最新的 CFR 报价和支付方式告知我们，并说明最快的交货日期及对定期订单的折扣政策。

7. You are kindly requested to quote the CIF Los Angels rate. 敬请将贵方 CIF 洛杉矶报价告知给我方。

本句中的"be kindly requested to"意思是"敬请"。

8. Owing to the fierce competition, it is important that your quotation would reach us not later than the end of this month so as not to miss the business chance. 由于市场竞争激烈，贵方最好在月底之前将报价通知给我们，以免错失商机。

本句中的"so as not to"引导目的状语。

Sentence Menu

1. **Opening**

    (1) We are importers in ... and would like to get in touch with suppliers of ... our company is ... and we specialize in the import and export of ...

    (2) We are engaged in/a dealer in ...

    (3) We have seen your advertisement in ... and should be glad if you would send us by return patterns and prices of good quality ... available from stock.

    (4) We have learned from ... that you are a leading manufacturer of plastic travel goods.

    (5) We were very much impressed by the quality and competitive pricing of your catering equipment shown at the recent Trade Fair in Paris, and feel that they could be marketed successfully in our country.

    (6) We are interested in your recently developed technology.

(7) We understand that you are manufacturers of . . . and should like to know whether you can supply . . .

2. Making requests

(1) As we are in the market for your . . . , we should be pleased if you would send us your best quotations.

(2) We have pleasure in enclosing our inquiry for . . . against which you are requested to make us an offer on CIF basis.

(3) Would you please provide information on the types and quality of . . . you have available, together with the prices?

(4) I would appreciate your sending me an up-to-date price list for your . . . products.

(5) We are prepared to purchase substantial quantity of . . . and shall appreciate your quoting us your bottom prices and acceptable terms of payments.

(6) We look forward to receiving your reply.

(7) We have learned that you are in a position to export . . . We are therefore writing to you and hope that you will send us a copy of the catalogue. In the meantime, please let us know the lowest price so that we can approach our clients for sales.

(8) We would appreciate your sending us a catalogue of . . . together with terms of payment and the largest discount you can allow us.

(9) One of our clients takes interest in your products and wishes to have your quotations for the items specified below.

(10) The articles we require are listed on the attached sheet. If you have them in stock, please tell us the quantity and also the lowest CFR Los Angeles price.

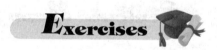

Exercises

I **Put the following terms or phrases from English into Chinese or vice versa.**

1. special price discount
2. latest price list
3. cash payment
4. pro forma invoice
5. in response to
6. pamphlet
7. 现货供应
8. 随函
9. 大宗交易
10. 经营范围
11. 货物已售
12. 操作指南

Unit 4 Inquiries

II **Fill in the blanks of the following letters with the words given below, and change the form when necessary.**

> oblige, inform, prefer, convince, discount, quantity, purchase, quotation, interest

Dear Sirs,

We are _____ to buy large quantity of corn and should be _____ if you would give us a _____ per metric ton FOB Los Angels, USA and _____ the earliest date you can ship.

We used to _____ corn from other sources, but we now _____ to buy from your corporation because we are given to the understanding that you are able to supply larger _____ with a special _____. Besides, we are _____ that your corn is of better quality.

We look forward to hearing from you by return.

Yours faithfully,

III **Complete the following sentences with the Chinese given in the brackets.**

1. The Showner Co. Ltd. informs us that you are _____ (最著名的男女针织套衫生产厂商).
2. We are _____ (随函附寄我方最新的图解目录和价格单) giving the details you asked for.
3. We would like to point out that we usually _____ (用即期信用证付款) which will be agreeable to you.
4. The illustrations will also give you _____ (我们其他出口产品的信息) in which you will be interested.
5. Our products are enjoying a high reputation in your area. Because of _____ (质优价廉), you can be sure they will _____ (帮您开拓市场).
6. If you _____ (有现货), please tell us the quantity and _____ (最低的 FOB 上海报价).
7. Some of our clients _____ (对贵方产品很感兴趣) and wish to _____ (得到贵方对以下产品的报价).
8. Shipment will be made within 3 weeks _____ (自接受订单日起).
9. As requested in your letter of February 27, 2015, we are now _____ (寄上形式发票一式四份) for our BCL Receiver T-34.

10. However, we have to point out that all the contents you fill in are _____ (对我方不具有任何约束性).

IV Writing practice.

Situational Writing

Suppose you were now working at Beijing Hardware Import and Export Co. Ltd and your company is going to import some hardware products from a Rome-based foreign company. **You are now requested to write an inquiry to the sales department of the foreign company, asking for data about quotation, discount, range of hardware products, and if necessary, the enclosure of the pricelist and catalogue.**

Unit 5

Quotations, Offers and Counter Offers

报盘与还盘

5.1 Quotations and Offers

5.1.1 Introduction

When a seller prepares to export, he or she quotes the customer the price of the goods on receipt of the inquiry. A quotation is a promise to supply goods on the terms stated and it generally includes all the necessary information requested. The prospective buyer is under no obligation to buy and the seller is not bound to sell. In brief, a quotation is not legally binding if the seller later decides not to sell. A satisfactory quotation will include the following:

(1) Thanks for the inquiry if there is any;
(2) The answers to all the information requested;
(3) Details of prices, terms of payment, and discounts;
(4) Additional information;
(5) Hope of orders or further inquiries.

An offer is made when a seller promises to sell goods at a stated price and within a stated period of time. The party sending the offer is called the offeror while another party is called offeree. An offer is mostly made in response to an inquiry, while it can also be voluntarily made by the seller to regular or new customers who may have interest in his or her products without any inquiry. If so, it is required to give an undertaking that all essential terms are clearly specified. A price quotation is not an offer due to lacking of expression of a promise to sell.

Some experts divide offer into two categories: firm offer and non-firm offer. A firm offer provides a period of validity and the acceptance made by the offeree before validity expires is effective legally, while a non-firm offer is unclear, incomplete and with reservations, and it is not binding on the offeror. Such expressions as *reference price*, *subject to our final confirmation*, and *subject to goods being unsold* are often employed in the non-firm offers. A firm offer should provide complete affirmative and specific terms of business, the beginning and the ending dates and the place of the validity.

Either for a quotation or an offer, the tone should be friendly and the language should be polite. As regards the structure, a quotation or an offer is generally divided into three parts. In the first part, the seller acknowledges the inquiry and expresses thanks for the customer's interest in his or her products. The second part presents the situation of stock, the terms and conditions and the validity (for a firm offer), while the hope that the quotation or the offer will be to the recipient's satisfaction and the expectation of an acceptance is expressed in the last part.

5.1.2 Letter Samples

 Letter 5-1 (A quotation for washing machines)

Dear Sirs,

We thank you very much for your letter of October 17, asking for our washing machines Model HTW 11 and Model HTW 14. We, as being requested, enclose our latest price list of this month and details of our conditions of sales and terms of payment.[1]

We have examined your proposal to place an order for a minimum number of our washing machines in return for a special allowance, but we feel it would be better to offer you a special allowance on the following sliding scale basis.

On purchases exceeding an annual total of:

US$10,000 but not exceeding US$20,000	1%
US$20,000 but not exceeding US$30,000	2%
US$30,000 but not exceeding US$40,000	3%
US$40,000 and above	4%

No special allowance could be given on annual total purchase below US$10,000.[2]

We feel that the above arrangement would be more satisfactory to both of us and can assure you that these goods are very popular in the European markets, of which we have had much experience.

We look forward to your acceptance of our proposal and to your orders.

Yours faithfully,

W. H. Ausman

Unit 5 Quotations, Offers and Counter Offers

 Letter 5-2（A quotation for down jackets）

Dear Sirs,

We thank you for your inquiry of September 23, and are pleased to send you our quotation for the goods you required as follows:

Commodity: "Polar Land" brand down jacket NFT13
Size: Large (L), medium (M), small (S)
Color: Brown, marine blue, yellow, green
Quantity: 800 pieces
Price: US$50.00 per piece CFR Philadelphia
Shipment: November

You are cordially invited to take advantage of this attractive quotation. We are anticipating a larger order from Canada, and that will cause a sharp rise in price.

We look forward to receiving your order.

Yours faithfully,

Lin Bing

 Letter 5-3（A non-firm offer for woolen mixed blankets）

Dear Sirs,

We have received your letter of November 11, asking us to offer you woolen mixed blankets. We are pleased to be told that there is a great demand for our products in Stockholm. In compliance with your request, we are making you the following offer subject to our final confirmation.[3]

Commodity: woolen mixed blankets, different colors and pattern assortment
Size: Large (L), medium (M) and small (S)
Packing: Blankets are wrapped in plastic bags and packed in standard cardboard cartons
Price: CFR Stockholm per dozen in US Dollars; L: 245, M: 235, S: 225
Payment: By irrevocable L/C payable by draft at sight

The Chinese woolen mixed blankets are of good quality and have fine workmanship and design.⁴ They are moderately priced, as known to all. You will certainly agree to that when you have examined our samples and quotation.

If you need any further information about our products, please let us know. We hope the above will be acceptable to you. We are looking forward to your order soon.

Yours faithfully,

Thomas Campion

 Letter 5-4 (A non-firm offer for cotton jackets)

Dear Sirs,

We thank you for your letter dated October 27, and are willing to enter into business relations with you on the basis of equality and mutual benefit. At your request, we take pleasure in making you a special offer, subject to our final confirmation, as follows:

Commodity: "Showner" brand cotton jackets NO. 33
Quantity: 500 dozens
Size: L/XL/XXL/XXXL
Color: White, red, yellow, blue
Price: US$2,000 per dozen CIF Sydney
Shipment: One month after receipt of L/C
Payment: By a 100% confirmed, irrevocable L/C in our favor payable by draft at sight to reach the sellers one month before shipment and remain valid for negotiation in China till the 15th day after shipment.⁵

We hope that the above will be acceptable to you and assure you of our best service at any time. We are looking forward to your prompt reply.

Yours faithfully,

John Chung

Unit 5 Quotations, Offers and Counter Offers

 Letter 5-5（A firm offer for corn and wheat）

Dear Sir or Madam,

We thank you for your letter dated December 7, asking us to make an offer for corn and wheat CIF Hongkong.

We e-mailed you this morning offering you 2,000 metric tons of corn at US＄137 per metric ton, CIF Hongkong, for shipment during May and June, 2015. This offer is subject to the receipt of your reply before April 15, 2015.

Please note that we have quoted our most favourable price and are unable to entertain any counter offer.

With regard to wheat, we have to tell you that all the lots we have now are under offer and we cannot supply from stock. However, if you make us a suitable offer, we may seek help from our supplying channels and there is still a possibility of supplying them to you.

There has been a heavy demand for corn and wheat in the last 3 months and this has resulted in increased prices. However, you may take advantage of the strengthening market if you send an early reply.

Yours faithfully,

Dirk Bogarde

 Letter 5-6（A firm offer for hard-nut crackers）

Dear Sirs,

We thank you for your fax of October 17 asking us to make firm offers for hard-nut cracker. We are pleased to know you are interested in our products.

We are offering you 500 sets of hard-nut crackers at US＄8 per set CFR Livorno or any other Italian main port for shipment during November/December, 2015.[6] This offer is firm, subject to receipt of reply by us before the end of October.

Please see to it that we have quoted our most favorable price and are unable to entertain any counter offer.

Our stock level on hand has been quite low, owing to heavy commitment, and we hope you can place an early order.

Yours faithfully,

Amy Lowell

Letter 5-7 (An offer for Dreamland-musician toys)

Dear Sirs,

Thank you for your letter of July 13, in which you asked for an offer from us for 10,000 sets of Dreamland-musician M-532 toys.

We are now making you the following offer: 10,000 sets of Dreamland-musician M-532 toys, at US$ 9.00 per set on FOB Shanghai basis for shipment in September 2006 with payment to be made by an irrevocable sight L/C.

We feel you may be interested in some of our other toys and therefore enclose our latest illustrated catalogue and a supply of sales literature for your reference.

We are looking forward to your order.

Yours faithfully,

Tom Liu

Unit 5　Quotations, Offers and Counter Offers

 Letter 5-8（**An offer for CD/VCD/MP3 players**）

Dear Sirs,

We have received your letter of March 17 and are pleased to make you the following offer subject to your reply reaching us by March 31, 2015.

Commodity: CD/VCD/MP3 player
Model: KW3739
Color: Blue
Quantity: 10,000 sets
Price: At US$ 87.00 each set FOB Tianjin
Shipment: In May
Payment: By L/C at sight to be opened through a bank acceptable to us

We are expecting large orders from importers in other countries and that will cause a sharp rise in price. Therefore, we hope you may take advantage of this attractive offer.

We look forward to your prompt reply.

Yours faithfully,

Arthur Xie

5.2　Counter Offers

5.2.1　Introduction

　　An offeree needs to make response to the offer he has received. Sometimes an offeree partly or totally disagrees with the offer but puts forward his own proposals and this is called a counter offer. If the offeree finds any terms or conditions in the offer unacceptable, he can negotiate with the seller and make a counteroffer to show his disagreement to the terms of payment, packing, shipment time, quantity or the date of delivery and state his own terms and conditions. In this case, the original offer is invalid, and the counter offer actually becomes a new offer from the original offeree. The original offerer or the seller now becomes the offeree and has the full right of acceptance or refusal. He may make a reply to the buyer's counter offer. This is called a counter-counter-offer. This process can go on for several rounds till business is concluded or called off.

In writing a counter offer, one has to state the terms most explicitly and use words carefully to avoid ambiguity or misunderstanding.[7] When a buyer rejects an offer, he should write to thank the seller and explain the reason for rejection. A letter of counter offer is usually composed of three parts. The first paragraph is designed to acknowledge the receipt of the offer and express the buyer's thanks. The explanation of the reasons to make the counter offer and the raised new terms and conditions are presented in the second part which can be divided into separate paragraphs. The buyer may use the last part to express his hope for a prompt reply or put forward his suggestions to do business together.

5.2.2 Letter Samples

Letter 5-9 (A counter offer for washing machines)

Dear Sirs,

We have received your offer of October 21 for 500 sets of washing machines Model HTW 11 and Model HTW 14 at US$ 35,000 with 3% discount.

In reply, we regret to inform you that the prices you quoted are found too high. We trust the quality of your products and would welcome the opportunity to do business with you. May we suggest that you give us more discount, say 5% on your quoted price of US$ 35,000? We believe that would help to introduce your goods to our market. Should you be prepared to grant us that rate of discount, we would be pleased to come to terms and place with you an order.

We are anticipating your early reply.

Yours faithfully,

W. Philips
Business Manager

Unit 5　Quotations, Offers and Counter Offers

 Letter 5-10（**A counter offer for down jackets**）

Dear Sirs,

We thank you for your offer of November 7, and the samples of "Polar Land" brand down jacket NFT13.

We know clearly that the quality of your jackets is very good, but we find your price is rather too high for our local market. Information indicates that the price of your products is around 20% higher than that of the Indonesia origin.

Such being the case, we have to ask you to consider if you can make a reduction in your price, say 15%. As our order would be no less than 800 pieces, you may think it worthwhile to make a concession. As the market is declining, we hope you will consider our proposal most favorably and fax us your acceptance, thus we may push the sales of your products.[8]

Yours faithfully,

William Carols

 Letter 5-11（**A reply to counter offer for down jackets**）

Dear Sirs,

We thank you very much for your letter of December 3, in which you asked us to reduce our price of "Polar Land" brand down jacket NFT13 by around 15%.

While appreciating your good wish to push the sales of our products, we regret to say that we cannot bring our price down to that low level at this stage. For your information, our "Polar Land" brand down jackets NFT13 have been well established in Netherlands, and there is a steady demand for them.

We trust it will not be difficult for our products to get a footing in your local market if you could see your way to do some marketing work. Please rest assured that we would always do our best to help you and promote the sales of our goods in your area.

Yours faithfully,

John Lesseter

Letter 5-12 (A counter offer for DVD players)

Dear Sirs,

We thank you for your fax offer of June 7 for 3,000 sets of Gloryfield brand DVD players. We appreciate the good quality of your goods, but unfortunately we are not in a position to accept the offer on your terms. Your prices are on rather high side.

To step up the trade, we suggest you make some concessions, say 4%, on your quoted prices, and we feel confident that it would help to push the sales of your goods in our market. If you can do so, we will place our order with you immediately. We hope you will not lose this chance so that you will benefit from this expanding market.

We will appreciate it very much if you could consider our counter offer most favorably and fax us your acceptance at your earliest convenience.

Yours faithfully,

Andrew Stanton

 Letter 5-13 (A counter offer for CD/VCD/MP3 players)

Dear Sirs,

We learn from your letter of June 12 that you offer us 10,000 sets of CD/VCD/MP3 player KW3739 at US$ 87.00 per set.

We regret to say that we find your price is rather high, and it will be difficult to convince our clients at your price.[9] We believe you are familiar with the market, and you cannot ignore the fierce competition from suppliers in Southeast Asian countries.

We suggest that you make some allowance, say 8% on your offered price. Since our order is large, it is worthwhile to make a concession. We hope you will consider our counter offer most favorably.

Look forward to your early reply.

Yours faithfully,

Andrew Stanton

Unit 5 Quotations, Offers and Counter Offers

 Letter 5-14（A counter offer for hiking boots）

Dear Sirs,

We note from your letter of April 23 that you are interested in our hiking boots but find that our offer of March 17 is a bit high.

We regret to say that we cannot comply with your request. To accept the prices you suggested would leave us little or no margin of profit on our sales. We have received many inquiries from importers in other countries and information shows that our price is fixed at a reasonable level.

We thank you again for your prompt response to our inquiry and offer, and would like to take this opportunity to conclude some transactions with you.

We are awaiting your early and favorable reply.

Yours faithfully,

Anna Ni

 Letter 5-15（A counter offer for hiking boots）

Dears Miss Anna,

Thank you for you letter of November 24, in which you asked us to reduce our prices by 10% on our water-proof hiking boots X-5. But regretfully enough, we are unable to entertain your counter offer, since your request of cutting the price by 10% will leave us no margin of profit on our sales.

However, on considering our long-term relations, we should like to make a concession and grant your request to lower the prices of our products. After careful study and consideration, we suggest a reduction of 6%, instead of the 10% you requested, should your order exceed 12,000 pairs.[10]

We are anticipating your prompt reply.

Yours sincerely,

Robert De Niro

Letter 5-16 (A counter offer for compasses)

Dear Sirs,

We have received your letter of August 7, informing us that you can supply us 15,000 AZ-3467 all-weather compasses at US$ 349.00 per set FOB Tokyo.

To be frank with you, we like the design and craftsmanship of your compasses, but your price is rather too high to be acceptable. As you know, the price of compasses has been declining in the last six months. We have to point out that manufacturers in other countries, including Republic of Korea, are actually lowering their prices according to a market survey made by us recently.

Due to this situation, it is impossible for us to accept your price. If you can make a reduction in you price, say 10%, we might come to terms.

We hope you will consider our counter offer most favorably and look forward to your early reply.

Yours faithfully,

Chazz Palminteri

Words and Vocabulary

binding	a.	有约束力的，附有义务的
undertaking	n.	事业，企业，承诺，保证
acceptance	n.	接受，承诺
polar	n.	极地，极
anticipate	v.	预测
negotiation	n.	议付
commitment	n.	许诺，承担义务
discount	n.	折扣
compass	n.	指南针，罗盘
counter offer		还盘

Unit 5 Quotations, Offers and Counter Offers

under no obligation	没有义务，没有责任
period of validity	有效期
subject to	服从
in compliance with	和……相符，和……一致
irrevocable letter of credit	不可撤销信用证
see to	保证，负责，注意
step up	逐步增加，提升，提高
comply with	和……相符，符合
margin of profit	盈利空间

Notes

1. We, as being requested, enclose our latest price list of this month and details of our conditions of sales and terms of payment.   我们按照贵方要求附上本月最新的价格单及详细的销售和支付条款。

   本句中的"as being requested"意思是"按照要求"。

2. No special allowance could be given on annual total purchase below US$ 10,000.
   年购买额低于 1 万美元，我们将不给予任何折让。

3. In compliance with your request, we are making you the following offer subject to our final confirmation.   应贵方要求我们按以下条款向贵方发盘，以我们最终的确认书为准。

   本句中的"subject to"意思是"以……为准，遵循……"。

4. The Chinese woolen mixed blankets are of good quality and have fine workmanship and design.
   中国混纺羊毛毛毯质量上乘，做工精良。

5. By a 100% confirmed, irrevocable L/C in our favor payable by draft at sight to reach the sellers one month before shipment and remain valid for negotiation in China till the 15th day after shipment.   以我方为受益人的 100% 保兑的、不可撤销的即期信用证于装运前 1 个月开抵卖方，并可于装运后 15 天内在中国议付。

   本句中的"in our favor"意思是"以我方为受益人的"，"negotiation"意为"议付"。

6. We are offering you 500 sets of hard-nut crackers at US$ 8 per set CFR Livorno or any other Italian main port for shipment during November/December, 2015.   我们按以下条款向贵方发盘：500 台坚果挤压机，每台 8 美元，CFR 里窝那或其他任何在 2015 年 11 月和 12 月期间装运的意大利港口。

7. In writing a counter offer, one has to state the terms most explicitly and use words carefully to avoid ambiguity or misunderstanding.   还盘时要清楚地写明各种条款，谨慎选词，以避免产生歧义或误解。

   本句中的"to state the terms"意思是"表述，陈述条款"。

8. As the market is declining, we hope you will consider our proposal most favorably and fax us

your acceptance, thus we may push the sales of your products. 鉴于市场疲软,希望贵方能同意我们的建议,并将接受函传真给我方,以促进贵方产品的销售。

本句中的 "push the sales" 意思是 "推销,促销"。

9. We regret to say that we find your price is high, and it will be difficult to convince our clients at your price. 很遗憾,我们发现贵方价格偏高,难以说服我们的客户接受。

本句中的 "regret to do..." 意思是 "遗憾地去做某事"。

10. After careful study and consideration, we suggest a reduction of 6%, instead of the 10% you requested, should your order exceed 12,000 pairs. 经过仔细研究和考虑,我们建议如下:如果贵方订单超过 12 000 双,我方将降价 6%,而非贵方所提出的 10%。

本句中的 "should" 引导一个条件状语从句,等于 "if your order exceeds..."。

Quotations and Offers

1. Opening

(1) Thank you for your letter of... in which you inquired about our range of...

(2) We thank you for your letter of..., and are pleased to enclose a detailed quotation for you.

(3) We appreciate your interest in...

2. Quoting prices and making offers

(1) We are pleased to inform you that our quotation is...

(2) We can allow you a special discount of... for orders exceeding... in value.

(3) If your order is valued at... we would allow you a special discount of...

(4) Our prices are quoted CIF...

(5) We have the pleasure to offer you... subject to our final confirmation.

(6) In regard to your request of... we are pleased to send you by separate parcel a copy of our sample products.

(7) You are kindly advised that we are sending you a special offer for the following goods in the hope that you will introduce them to prospective buyers at your end.

(8) This offer is open until...

(9) This is the most reasonable price we can offer at present, and any further reduction on our side is out of the question.

(10) On condition that you take more than..., we are prepared to offer this special price of...

(11) We shall book a trial order with you, provided you will give us a... discount.

Unit 5 Quotations, Offers and Counter Offers

Counter offers

1. Opening

(1) In reply to your letter of offer, we regret to say that our customers here find your price rather high and above the prevailing market level.

(2) We feel regretful for inability to accept your offer.

(3) We are sorry that we cannot take advantage of your firm offer this time.

(4) Unfortunately, we cannot accept your request.

(5) Much to our regret, we are unable to entertain your offer because the ... you quoted do not meet our clients' requirement.

(6) We regretfully learn from your letter that your present price is ... % higher than ...

2. Making counter offers

(1) Owing to the heavy commitment of our manufacturer, we are unable to entertain fresh booking for the moment.

(2) According to our investigation, the market is now showing a decline, so we are expecting an adjustment of the price at the end of this month.

(3) We hope this counter offer will meet your approval and we shall place regular orders with you on receipt of your confirmation.

(4) The best we can do is to make a reduction of ... % in our previous quotation.

(5) This new model of machine has all the qualities of the one you asked for, and it has added advantage of being lighter, stronger and more durable.

(6) We counteroffer as follows:

(7) This is our rock-bottom price; we cannot make any further reduction.

(8) The offer we obtained recently from other sources for the same product is around ... % below yours.

(9) We have cut price to the limit. We regret, therefore, being unable to comply with your request for further reduction.

(10) Should you be ready to reduce your price by, say ... %, we might conclude terms.

I Put the following terms or phrases from English into Chinese or vice versa.

1. market survey
2. make a concession
3. validity
4. margin of profits

5. binding on
6. firm offer
7. 减价 7%
8. 副本
9. 及时装运
10. 试订单
11. 达成协议
12. 提出建议

II Fill in the blanks of the following letters with the words given below, and change the form when necessary.

> follow, arrive, pay, commodity, discount, ship, minimum, expand, acknowledge, please

Dear Sirs,

We are very _____ to receive your inquiry of November 24 and _____ your interest in our products. We confirm our fax of this morning as _____:

_____: handmade cotton embroidered gloves

_____: by L/C at sight

_____: within 5-6 weeks after the _____ of the L/C

We feel sure you will realize that our quoted price is very reasonable. However, in order to help you to _____ your new business, we are prepared to allow you a special _____ of 5% if your _____ quantity order is not less than 10,000 pairs.

Yours faithfully,

III Rearrange the following sentences in logic order to make them a perfect letter.

1. It is known that our products are superior in quality and moderate in price, and are very popular in the international market. We hope you will agree to our offer.
2. As Christmas is approaching, please send us your orders without any delay.
3. Thank you for your inquiry of November 23 for Christmas trees.
4. Your prompt reply will be highly appreciated.
5. As requested, we are offering Model 325 plastic trees you require at US$ 478 per dozen CIFC 1.5% Copenhagen subject to our final confirmation.

Unit 5 Quotations, Offers and Counter Offers

IV Translate the following letter into English.

敬启者：

  我们非常感谢你方 10 月 29 日的询盘，并高兴地获悉你方愿与我们建立贸易关系。按照要求，现向你方报盘如下，你方答复于 2015 年 11 月 24 日前到达我地有效。

  规格："秀奈尔"牌男式睡衣
  数量：3 万套
  价格：CFR 米兰价，每套 40 美元
  支付：保兑的，不可撤销的凭即期汇票支付的信用证
  装运：从 2016 年 1 月

  我方相信上述条件能为你方同意。市价很可能会上涨，尽早订购对你方有利。希望早日收到你方订单。

V Translate the following letter into Chinese.

Dear Mr. Smith,

Thank you for your letter of October 6th, 2015 in which you requested about our product Electric Saws BNT-3.

While the specifications of the product are enclosed, our commercial terms such as price and shipping and payment terms are indicated as follows:

Quantity: 100 units
Price: US$ 100.00 per unit, CIF New York
Payment Terms: L/C to be established within one week after order
Shipment: within one month after receipt of L/C

We hope the above quotations are of interest to you and we are looking forward to getting your reply soon.

Sincerely yours,

VI Writing practice.

Situational Writing 1

Write a firm offer covering the following contents.

- 毛皮手套
- 颜色有黑、棕、红3种
- 材料选用优质羊皮
- 价格：CFR 大连价，13 美元一副
- 由装船前 30 天开立的保兑的，不可撤销的即期信用证支付
- 包装由买方决定
- 10 月船期

Situational Writing 2

Write a letter with the following hints.

- Thanks for inquiry
- Making an offer
- Commodity：" Butterfly" brand bed sheet TN7032
- Price：at US$ 478 Per dozen
- Packing：one dozen per box, 12 boxes per carton
- Payment：by confirmed, irrevocable L/C payable by draft at sight
- Expectation of favorable reply

Unit 6

Orders and Acknowledgements
订购与确认

6.1 Introduction

    The order from a buyer is an offer to buy. Going through inquiry, quotation and several rounds of offer and counter[1], the seller and the buyer come to an agreement and the buyer may place an order with the seller. An order can be sent by a letter, a printed form order, a fax or an email message. Usually well-known customers will probably use a form while a new customer or one placing a single order often writes a letter.[2]

    No matter what forms the buyer may choose, the order must be accurate, clear, specific and complete. The buyer must make the seller know clearly the exact goods he wants. The language of an order letter should be definite, exact and simple. Experiences show it is important that the buyer should pay special attention to spelling and any decimal point.[3] The writer is strongly recommended to double check all price calculations to avoid making mistakes before sending the letter.

    An order may include the descriptions of the following specific items:

(1) Name of commodity;
(2) Quality requirements and specifications;
(3) Quantity;
(4) Price;
(5) Packing and marking;
(6) Terms of delivery;
(7) Terms of payment;
(8) Documents.

    A letter of order is mostly composed of three parts. The buyer prepares the first part to refer to the previous contact, and describes the details of the order in the second part, followed by the last part that states the terms and form of payment, the anticipated date of delivery and the mode of transportation.

    Upon receipt of an order, the seller should acknowledge it in good time.[4] If the goods ordered are available, the seller had better lose no time to state his acknowledgement and repeat the terms in the letter of order. The seller, in the acknowledgement, may praise the buyer for his or her wise order, express thanks to longtime customer or deliver a hearty welcome to a new customer. Quite often a letter of acknowledgement includes the following contents:

(1) Acknowledgement of the order with expressions of thanks;

(2) Restatement of the shipping instructions and the terms of payment;

(3) Favorable comments on the goods ordered;

(4) Recommendation of other products likely to be of interest;

(5) Hope for further orders.

When the seller cannot accept an order because the goods required are out of stock or the price and the specifications have been changed, he or she should write a rejecting letter with utmost care immediately so as to alleviate or eliminate the negative impact on future business with the customer.[5]

6.2 Letter Samples

 Letter 6-1 (An order for peanuts)

Dear Sirs,

We have received your letter of March 7 and now place an order with you at your revised price: "Fifty metric tons of Peanuts at US$700 per metric ton CFR Dalian for shipment in May."

Enclosed is our Purchase Confirmation NO. 137 in duplicate.[6] Please sign and return one copy for our records at your earliest convenience.

We are arranging for the establishment of the covering letter of credit and shall let you know by fax as soon as it is opened.

We stress the importance of making punctual shipment within the validity of the L/C, and any delay in shipment would be harmful to our future business.[7]

Yours faithfully,

Liu Guanru

Unit 6 Orders and Acknowledgements

 Letter 6-2（An order for hiking shoes）

Dear Sirs,

Thank you for your offer of October 11 for hiking shoes and the samples you sent us.

Having examined your samples carefully, we found the quality of materials used, the prices and the workmanship are up to our requirement.[8] We are pleased to send you an order for the following items on the understanding that they will be supplied at the prices mentioned.

500 pairs of men's hiking shoes
Size and quantity: 40 (100 pairs), 41 (100 pairs), 42 (200 pairs), 43 (100 pairs), each pair at US$140 CIF Shanghai

400 pairs of women's hiking shoes
Size and quantity: 39 (50 pairs), 38 (100 pairs), 37 (150 pairs), 36 (100 pairs), each pair at US$125 CIF Shanghai

Our order is subject to your acceptance of our usual terms of payment, i.e. cash against documents.

We expect to find a good market for the above and hope to place further and larger orders with you.

Yours faithfully,

Ross Liang

 Letter 6-3（An order for hard-nut crackers）

Dear Sirs,

Subject: Hard-nut crackers

We have received your letter of November 8, and are satisfied with your quotation for the hard-nut crackers and have decided to place a trial order for them on the terms stated in your letter.

As the Christmas season is coming and the goods are urgently needed, we hope the shipment can be made before December 1. Our order is simply stated as follows:

Quantity	Model	Price
3,000	HB-3	US$15,000

We suggest payment by 100% confirmed and irrevocable letter of credit in your favor, payable by draft at sight. Please let us know if this is agreeable to you.

We are pleased to have transacted this initial business with you and look forward to further expansion of trade to our mutual benefit.[9]

Yours faithfully,

Aldolf Smith

  Letter 6-4 (An order for machine tools)

Dear Sirs,

We have received your letter of January 3 and thank you for the catalogue and price list enclosed. We are satisfied with the quality and specifications of your products after we studied the pamphlets.

We are sending you one copy of our sales confirmation NO. 4345 placing an order with you for your machine tools with the value totaling US$85,000. As these goods are urgently needed, please make shipment of the goods before the end of February.

We will instruct our bank to open our confirmed irrevocable L/C in your favor the moment we receive your confirmation on the order.

There is a great demand for machine tools in our market, and the subsequent orders will be in large quantities. We are looking forward to your early reply and confirmation.

Yours faithfully,

Robert De Niro

Unit 6 Orders and Acknowledgements

  Letter 6-5(An order for lamps)

Dear Sirs,

Subject: TM-T12 Lamps

Further to our discussions through fax and e-mail, we should like to confirm details of ordering the subject goods:

Quantity	Description	Amount
6,000 sets	TM-T12 Lamps	US$150,000.00

The above price are quoted on CFR Dalian basis.

Packing: Each set in a box, 12 sets to a cardboard carton and 60 sets to a wooden case.
Shipment: To be made in three equal monthly installments, beginning from June, 2015.
Payment: By confirmed, irrevocable L/C payable by draft at 60 days sight to be opened 30 days before the time of shipment.

We would like you to send us your acknowledgement of this order as soon as possible. When we receive your acknowledgement, we will arrange to apply for L/C.

We look forward to your reply.

Yours faithfully,

Arthur Doyle

  Letter 6-6(An order for transistor radios)

Dear Sirs,

We confirm our agreement on purchase of the following goods:

Description of Article: "Satect" brand transistor radio
Model: GML-268 Hi-sensitivity 9-band receiver
Quantity: 4,800 sets

Price: US$55.00 per set CIF Rabat
Packing: Each set is packed in a polybag then in a box, 12 sets to a cardboard carton and 96 sets to a wooden case.
Delivery: As we need the goods urgently, please deliver them within 40 days after receipt of the order.
Payment: By irrevocable documentary letter of credit opened through Bank of China and drawn at sight.
Shipping marks: Mark the cases with our initials TNS in a circle, under which comes the destination RABAT with order number SY 2356 below again.[10]

We trust that you will give special care to the packing of the goods lest they should be damaged in transit.

Yours faithfully,

Chazz Palminteri

 Letter 6-7 (An acknowledgement letter of an order for transistor radios)

Dear Sirs,

Thank you for your Order NO. 2356 for GML-268 Hi sensitivity 9-band receivers and assure you that all the items you required are in stock.

We confirm with you the following order for transistor radios at the prices stated in your letter of October 14.

Description of article: "Satect" brand transistor radio
Model: GML-268 Hi-sensitivity 9-band receiver
Quantity: 4800 sets
Price: US$55.00 per set CIF Rabat
Packing: Each set is packed in a polybag then in a box, 12 sets to a cardboard carton and 96 sets to a wooden case.
Delivery: Deliver within 40 days after receipt of the order.
Payment: By irrevocable documentary letter of credit opened through Bank of China and drawn at sight.

Shipping marks: Mark the cases with your initials TNS in a circle, under which comes the destination RABAT with order number SY 2356 below again.

For the above order, we enclose our Purchase Confirmation NO. 1578 in duplicate. Please sign and return one copy for our file at your earliest convenience.

Thank you again for your order.

Yours faithfully,

Michael Blevins

 Letter 6-8 (An acknowledgement letter of an order for washing machines)

Dear Sirs,

Thank you very much for your order for our SC-Y12 full-automatic washing machines, and it draws our immediate attention.

The prices and terms of payment you suggested are acceptable, and you may rely on us to give your order prompt attention. We will arrange shipment accordingly and shall send you the shipping advice and the invoice at the time of shipment by the end of July.

We are working on your order and will keep you informed in time of the progress.

I am sure you will be pleased to collect good comments about our products from your consumers, and build up a market for the product in your region.

Yours faithfully,

Carlos M. Luis

Letter 6-9(An order for washing machines)

Dear Sirs,

In reply to your counter offer of September 23, we are sending you this confirming letter and are pleased to place an order with you as follows:

Commodity: "Super Cleaner" brand washing machine
Model: AZ-6732
Quantity: 10,000 sets
Price: US$386.00 per set
Delivery: By the end of October
Packing: In firm, plastic-lined, waterproof cases
Payment: Draft at sight under irrevocable L/C

Since we are in urgent need of the above goods, please confirm this order by return. We expect to find a good market for washing machines and hope to place further and large orders with you in the near future if this initial order turns out to be satisfactory.

Yours faithfully,

Stanley Kubrick

 Letter 6-10(A confirming letter for an order for hiking boots)

Dear Sirs,

We have pleasure in receiving your order and would like to thank you for your cooperation and assistance rendered to us. We are confident that you will be satisfied with our service and the quality of our goods.

We confirm that the X-7 all-weather hiking boots you ordered are in stock and can be supplied at the prices stated in your letter of July 8. Enclosed is our Sales Confirmation No. 438 in duplicate, a copy of which is to be countersigned and returned for our records.

It is understood that a letter of credit in our favor covering the above mentioned goods will be established immediately.¹¹ We wish to point out that the stipulations in the relevant credit should strictly conform to the terms stated in our Sales Confirmation in order to avoid subsequent amendments.

Your prompt reply and the related L/C at the earliest date will be appreciated.

Yours faithfully,

John Clive

Words and Vocabulary

order	n.	订单
description	n.	种类，描述
packing	n.	包装
marking	n.	记号，标志，唛头
document	n.	单据
acknowledge	v.	认可，承认
restatement	n.	再声明，重述
alleviate	v.	减轻，缓解
eliminate	v.	排除，消除
duplicate	n.	一式两份
punctual	a.	准时的
hiking	n.	徒步旅行
cracker	n.	粉碎机
transact	v.	办理，交易
pamphlet	n.	小册子
initial	n.	词首大写字母
invoice	n.	发票
plastic-lined	a.	塑料压边的，塑料衬里的
waterproof	a.	防水的
countersign	n.	会签，副署

form order	格式订单
well-known customer	知名客户
decimal point	小数点
double check	双重检查
quality requirements	质量要求
terms of delivery	交货条件
mode of transportation	运输方式
longtime customer	老客户
purchase confirmation	购货确认书
cash against documents	见单即付
sales confirmation	销售确认书
cardboard carton	硬纸盒,纸板箱
wooden case	木箱
Hi-sensitivity 9-band receiver	高灵敏度9波段收音机
polybag	塑料袋
shipping advice	装船通知
initial order	首笔订单

Notes

1. Going through inquiry, quotation and several rounds of offer and counter... 经过询盘、报价及几轮发盘和还盘……
   本句中的"round"意思是"回合,轮次"。

2. Usually well-known customers will probably use a form while a new customer or one placing a single order often writes a letter. 通常老客户用格式订单,而新客户或单一订单客户则采用信件的形式。

3. Experiences show that it is important that the buyer should pay special attention to spelling and any decimal point. 经验表明,买方留意拼写和小数点是很重要的。

4. Upon receipt of an order, the seller should acknowledge it in good time. 收到订单后,卖方应及时确认。
   本句中的"upon"意思是"当……时候,一……就……","in good time"意为"非常及时"。

5. ... he or she should write a rejecting letter with utmost care immediately so as to alleviate or eliminate the negative impact on future business with the customer. ……应立即谨慎地写一封拒绝信,以减轻或消除由此对客户未来贸易关系所产生的消极影响。

6. Enclosed please find our Purchase Confirmation NO. 137 in duplicate. 随信附上我方购货确认书，编号为137，一式两份。

   本句中的"in duplicate"意思是"一式两份"。

7. We stress the importance of making punctual shipment within the validity of the L/C, and any delay in shipment would be harmful to our future business. 我们强调在信用证有效期内按时装运，任何方式的延迟装运都将损害我们未来的业务合作。

8. Having examined your samples carefully, we found the quality of materials used, the prices and the workmanship are up to our requirement. 我们详细研究过贵方样品后，发现贵方的产品价格、所采用的原材料及做工都能满足我们的要求。

   本句中的"up to ... requirement"意为"达到……的水平或要求"。

9. We are pleased to have transacted this initial business with you and look forward to further expansion of trade to our mutual benefit. 很高兴和贵方做成这第一笔生意，希望在互利的基础上进一步扩大我们之间的贸易。

   本句中的"to our mutual benefit"意为"对双方有利，互利"。

10. Mark the cases with our initials TNS in a circle, under which comes the destination RABAT with order number SY 2356 below again. 在木箱上标注我公司的首字母缩写TNS，并将其放在圆圈内，然后在其下面注明运输目的地RABAT。最下面是我方的订单编号SY 2356。

    本句中的"circle"意为"圆圈，圆"，"order number"的意思是"订单编号"。

11. It is understood that a letter of credit in our favor covering the above mentioned goods will be established immediately. 敬请贵方立即根据上述货物开立以我方为受益人的信用证。

Sentence Menu

1. Placing orders

(1) We are pleased to enclose an order we have received from ... for ...

(2) We place this order on the understanding that the consignment is dispatched by ... and that we reserve the right to cancel it and to refuse delivery after the date.

(3) Reference is made to exchange of correspondence between us, and we confirm having placed with you the following order:

(4) In reply, we wish to order from you the items in your quotation and will apply for governmental approval to import them.

(5) We confirm our agreement on purchase of the following goods:

(6) We find both quality and prices satisfactory and we are pleased to give you an order for the following items on the understanding that they will be supplied from stock at the prices mentioned.

(7) Your samples of . . . have received favorable reaction from our clients, and we are pleased to enclose our order for . . .

(8) We have the pleasure of sending you an order for . . . at US$ . . .

(9) The particulars are detailed in the enclosed order sheet No. . . .

(10) As we are in urgent need of the goods, we find it necessary to stress the importance of making punctual shipment within validity of L/C.

2. Acknowledging orders

(1) We have duly received your Sales Contract No. . . .

(2) Your compliance will be appreciated.

(3) We are very pleased to receive your order and confirm that all the items required are in stock.

(4) We are very much obliged for your trial order of . . . for . . .

(5) We have pleasure in informing you that we have booked your order No. . . . for . . . We are sending you our Sales Confirmation No. . . . in duplicate, one copy of which please sign and return for our file.

(6) You may rest assured that this order will have our careful attention.

(7) We are sure you will be pleased to collect good comments about our products from your customers, and build up a market for the product in your region.

(8) We appreciate your cooperation and look forward to receiving your further orders.

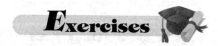

Exercises

I Put the following terms or phrases from English into Chinese or vice versa.

1. double check
2. shipping advice
3. sales contract
4. form order
5. cardboard carton
6. process the order
7. 付款交单
8. 推荐合适的替代产品
9. 首笔订单
10. 一式两份
11. 需求增长
12. 延迟装运

II Fill in the blanks of the following letters with the words given below, and change the form when necessary.

> inform, full, comment, lead, through, sure, for, receive, arrange, work

Unit 6 Orders and Acknowledgements

Dear Sirs,

We have _____ with thanks your order _____ 1 M/Ts of tea. We are _____ on your order and will keep you _____ in time of the progress.

We are expecting to _____ the establishment of the related Confirmed Irrevocable Letter of Credit _____ the bankers.

Since it is the best season for tea, we hope you make _____ use of the opportunity. I am _____ you will be pleased to collect good _____ about our tea from your consumers.

We hope this will _____ to more considerable orders.

Yours faithfully,

III Compare the following two letters and point out why the revision is made so.

A. The Original Letter

Dear Lucy,

We would like to change our order of the plastic Christmas trees which I sent you November 23 due to the increasing demand for them here. Although the order of 7,000 plastic Christmas trees is very large, more people want to purchase. So please send 3,000 more CT732 Christmas plastic trees. We are sorry to confuse you.

As the Christmas is coming, please give careful attention to our change.

Awaiting your prompt reply.

Yours faithfully,

Louis

B. The Revised Letter

Dear Lucy,

We would like to make a change in our order of November 23.

Would you please send 3,000 more CT732 Christmas plastic trees? The reason is that your products enjoy great popularity here, and there is an increasing demand for them.

Since the Christmas is coming, could you please make the shipment by the end of this month?

Looking forward to your reply.

Yours sincerely,

Louis

Ⅳ Translate the following letter into Chinese.

Dear Sirs,

We thank you for your letter of November 8 with which you enclosed your pricelist and catalogue.

We agree that the quality is up to the standard and the prices you quoted are satisfactory. We also note that you will allow us a discount of 3% on an order worth US$30,000 or more. We, therefore, have airmailed you our Order No. 879 on November 6.

Please note that as these goods are urgently required here, we should be most grateful if you could dispatch the goods as soon as possible.

Yours faithfully,

Ⅴ Translate the following letter into English.

敬启者:

兹高兴地确认按照下列条款买进你方德声（TECSUN）9波段收音机4 000台。

4 000 台德声 9 波段收音机，上海成本、保险加运费价格，每台 53 美元。收到信用证 14 天内，从上海运至孟买。

请特别注意货物的包装，以免货物在运输途中受损。

我们现在正在申请办理信用证，在接到你方确认书后，即可开出以你方为受益人的信用证。

谨上

2015 年 12 月 5 日

Ⅵ Writing practice.

Situational Writing

Write a letter with the following given particulars.

- 确认收到卖方寄来的样品，表示感谢。
- 订购 2 000 台尼康 D80 数码相机。
- 要求迅速发货。
- 随信附上 678 号购买确认书，一式两份。

Unit 7

Payment by Letter of Credit
信用证付款

7.1 Introduction

Letter of credit is the most commonly used means of payment in international trade, as it can ensure that an exporter gets his money when he dispatches his goods — not when they are received by the customer, thus giving the exporter the largest possible protection.

The procedure for a letter of credit begins with completion of the contract. When a contract of transaction is signed, the buyer is usually under obligation to establish a letter of credit with his bank within the time stipulated in the sales contract (confirmation). However, there may be circumstances where the buyer fails to establish L/C, or it does not reach the seller in time; then a letter, a fax or whatever media is considered safe and quick has to be used to urge buyer to expedite the L/C or to give notification of its whereabouts. When urging establishment of L/C, the first message conveyed should be polite, indicating that the goods ordered are ready but the relevant L/C has not yet arrived. If the first message has no response from the buyer, a second one will be sent, though still restrained in tone, to let the recipient feel your disappointment and concerns.

When the seller finds that there are some discrepancies or some unforeseen special clauses to which he or she does not agree in the L/C, the seller should send an advice to the buyer, asking him or her to make an amendment to the L/C. Sometimes an unexpected event may take place to goods supply, shipment, etc, which will require timely amendment to the original L/C.

Not only can the seller ask for amendment to an L/C, the buyer can likewise ask for amendment if he or she finds something in the L/C needs to be altered. The usual procedure is that the buyer should first obtain consent from the seller and then instruct the opening bank to amend the L/C. The request for L/C amendment is usually made by fax or even email.

Besides the date of shipment, which is usually stipulated in the L/C, every L/C has its expiry date. In order to leave sufficient time to the seller to make out the shipping documents and the bank to make their negotiation, the date of shipment and the expiry date of the L/C should be made at least two weeks apart.

Sometimes the seller may fail to get the goods ready for shipment in time or the buyer may request that the shipment be postponed for one reason or another; then the seller will have to ask for extension of the expiry date as well as the date of shipment of the L/C.

If the beneficiary is satisfied with the credit or the amendment to the credit, he arranges for the goods to be shipped. Meanwhile, he prepares the documents in accordance with the credit. Of all the documents, the more essential is the bill of exchange, which the exporter draws on the issuing bank. The bill of exchange is made payable at sight or within certain days after sight, according to the credit. Besides, other documents the exporter will have to prepare under a letter of credit include commercial invoice, the packing list and any other documents the importer specifies in the L/C.

After the goods have been shipped and the bill of lading has been obtained, the beneficiary delivers all the documents to the negotiating bank with the credit. The bank checks the documents against the credit. If it is satisfied that they are in order, the bank pays the beneficiary right away, in case the accompanying draft is payable at sight, or within a certain period of time after sight, in case the credit is accompanied by a time draft.

When the applicant's bank has ascertained that all the instructions in the credit are complied with, it pays its correspondent, debits the L/C amount to the applicant's account in the manner agreed on, and releases the documents.[1] With these, the importer is able to take delivery of the goods covered by the L/C.

7.2 Letter Samples

 Letter 7-1 (Asking for opening the L/C)

Dear Sir or Madam,

We shall be very glad if you will arrange to open an irrevocable letter of credit for US$16,200 in favor of the Qingdao Trading Company, the credit to be valid until September 3. Enclosed is an application form for documentary credit.

The credit which evidences shipment of 5,000 cases of cutlery may be used against presentation of the following documents:[2] Bills of Lading in triplicate, one copy of Commercial Invoice, Packing List, Certificate of Insurance and Certificate of Origin. The company may draw on your New York office at 90 days for each shipment.

Yours faithfully,

Susan Block
Manager

Letter 7-2(Asking for opening the L/C)

Dear Mr. Gao,

Please open an Irrevocable Letter of Credit for US$ 40,000 in favor of the Medic Medical Equipment Ltd., the credit to be valid until October 30.

The documents, which may be used against negotiation, are as follows: Bills of Lading, Commercial Invoice and Packing List in triplicate.

The conditions of shipment of 400 sets of medical equipment are as per S/C No. 987: Transshipment is prohibited and partial shipments are permitted.[3]

We enclose the application form for the L/C and would be pleased if you can open the L/C as soon as possible.

Yours sincerely,

Wang Wei
Manager

 Letter 7-3(Urging establishment of L/C)

Dear Sirs,

With reference to the 5,000 dozen shirts under our Sales Confirmation No. 504, we would like you to know that the date of delivery is approaching, but up to the present we have not received the covering Letter of Credit. Please do your utmost to expedite its establishment so that we may process the order as agreed.

In order to avoid subsequent amendment, please see to it that the L/C stipulations should be in strict conformity with the terms of the contract.

We look forward to receiving your favorable response earlier.

Yours faithfully,

Liu Yun
Manager

Letter 7-4（Urging establishment of L/C）

Dear Mr. Bemstein,

As of today, we have not received your L/C covering 3,000 TAMs you are buying from us. Please check your Purchase Contract #AS-166 and you will see that you have promised to open the covering credit before the end of August. Are you having some problem that we can help you with?

Your order has been made up for quite some time and on the other hand, the demand for our products has been extremely great recently. Mr. Benstein, we hope you can understand that we cannot afford to keep the goods for you too long.

For your benefit, please expedite the L/C, which must reach us before September 18.

If this is not feasible, please call or write me today. Thank you.

Sincerely yours,

Zhou Qiang
Export Manager

 Letter 7-5（Amendment to L/C）

Dear Mr. Oscar,

We thank you for L/C No. 378 for 20 M/T of crabs against S/C No. EX55. But much to our regret, there are two discrepancies between the L/C and the S/C. Hereby we list them below for your attention:

1. It is stipulated in our S/C No. EX55 that shipment should be made on or before 31st of October, but the L/C states: "latest shipment date: 20th of October, 2015".

2. Our S/C states, partial shipment and transshipment allowed, whereas the L/C says that transshipment is prohibited.

We would like you to make the above-mentioned amendments immediately.

We won't be able to ship the goods in time if the amendments come too late.

We are waiting for your quick reply.

Sincerely yours,

Cheng Gang
Manager

 Letter 7-6（Amendment to the L/C）

Dear Oscar,

We have received your letter of credit No. 395, under S/C No. EX56. On examination, we find two points, which do not conform to the stipulations of S/C No. EX56.

Please amend the L/C as follows:

The total value of your order should be US$250,000 instead of US$150,000.

Add the wording: "five percent more or less allowed" after the number of the quantity.

Your prompt attention to this matter will be highly appreciated.

Yours sincerely,

Cheng Qiang
Manager

 Letter 7-7（Amendment to the L/C）

Dear Mr. Crane,

Thank you for your L/C No. NBN99876 issued by the National Bank of Bangladesh, which arrived here yesterday.

On going through the L/C, however, we found the product specified in it is Model UX166 instead of Model UX106 as contracted.

We are able to supply UX166 in the quality you require in case you really wish to have this model. You may refer to the catalogue we previously sent you and will find that UX166 has more functions than UX106, but the price is only US$5.00 higher per set.

You are, therefore, requested to amend the L/C in question[4] either by rewriting the Model Number to read UX106; or by increasing the aggregate amount to US$110,000 and the unit price to US$55.00 CIF Dhaka.

Please let us have your L/C amendment advice next week so that we may effect shipment within the contracted delivery time. Thank you.

Sincerely yours,

Zhang Fen
Export Manager

 Letter 7-8 (Requesting extension of L/C)

Dear Sirs,

With reference to your L/C No. 4938 covering 3,000 cases of iron nails, we regret to inform you that it is impossible for us to fulfill the shipment before the end of September, as the earliest steamer sailing for your port is scheduled to leave Shanghai around October 2 and the next ship, as we were told, will be sailing late October or early November.

Such being the case, we have to ask you to extend the shipment date and validity of your L/C to November 15 and November 30 respectively[5] and see to it that the amendment advice reaches us by October 1.

Your prompt attention to this matter will be highly appreciated.

Faithfully yours,

Zhang Ming,
Manager

Letter 7-9 (Requesting extension of L/C)

Dear Sirs,

We refer to your Order No.123 for 50 tons of fish.

Owing to problems at the port and our shipping company, we will not be able to meet the stipulated delivery date of December 30.

We expect that we will be able to meet Jan. 20th, 2016 delivery deadline, so would you please make an extension for the L/C?

We apologize for the inconvenience, but the delay due to circumstances is beyond our control.

Yours faithfully,

Cheng Fang

Words and Vocabulary

expedite	v.	加快
restrained	a.	克制的，有所保留的
discrepancy	n.	不符，差异
unforeseen	a.	不可预见的
amendment	n.	修改
consent	n.	同意
expiry	n.	满期，(期限)终止
beneficiary	n.	受益人
correspondent	n.	通信者
evidence	v.	证明
triplicate	n.	一式三份
covering	a.	相关的，有关的
subsequent	a.	随后的，以后的
aggregate	a.	总的，全部的

Unit 7 Payment by Letter of Credit

validity	n.	有效性
advice	n.	通知
deadline	n.	最后期限
Letter of Credit		信用证
the packing list		装箱单
the application form		申请表
as of		自……起，到……为止
in question		有关的

Notes

1. When the applicant's bank has ascertained that all the instructions in the credit are complied with, it pays its correspondent, debits the L/C amount to the applicant's account in the manner agreed on, and releases the documents. 当开证申请人的银行（开证行）确认，信用证中所有的指示都与随附单据相符，该银行便对其往来行进行偿付，以事先约定的方式将信用证中的金额记入开证申请人账户的借方。

   本句中的"debit...to one's account"意为"借记某人的账户"，即"从其人的账上提取"，与debit（记入借方）相对的是credit（记入贷方）。

2. The credit which evidences shipment of 5,000 cases of cutlery may be used against presentation of the following documents： 下列单据可以与载明5 000箱餐刀的信用证一起使用。

   本句中介词"against"为"与……对比"，"与……对照"的意思。

3. The conditions of shipment of 400 sets of medical equipment are as per S/C No. 987: Transshipment is prohibited and partial shipments are permitted. 400套医疗设备的运输条件可以参照第987号销售确认书上的规定。

   本句的"as per"为法律用语，意为"依据，参照"。

4. You are, therefore, requested to amend the L/C in question... 因此，我们请求你方修改该信用证……

   本句中"in question"的意思为"正被谈论的"，例如"the book in question"意为"该书"。

5. Such being the case, we have to ask you to extend the shipment date and validity of your L/C to November 15 and November 30 respectively... 鉴于如此情况，我们不得不要求你方延长运输期限并将信用证的有效期分别改为11月15日和11月30日……

   本句中的"such being the case"为独立结构，其中such是主语，"being the case"是现在分词，表示原因。

Sentence Menu

1. Asking for opening L/C

(1) Please see to it that payment is made by confirmed, irrevocable letter of credit in our favor, available by draft at sight, and allowing transshipment and partial shipments.

(2) As agreed, we only require 100% value, confirmed and irrevocable L/C payable at sight.

(3) With regard to terms of payment, we regret being unable to accept D/P terms, we insist on the terms of L/C.

(4) Under relevant L/C, your draft should be accompanied by a complete set of shipping documents, and other documents consisting of . . .

2. Urging establishment of L/C

(1) As the goods against your Order No. . . . have been ready for quite some time, it is imperative that you take immediate action to have the covering L/C established as soon as possible.

(2) The date of delivery of your Order No. . . . is approaching, but we still have not received the covering L/C up to date. Please do your utmost to expedite the L/C to reach us before . . . so that shipment may be effected without delay.

(3) Please do your utmost to expedite the covering L/C, so that we may execute the order smoothly.

(4) We regret that up to now we haven't received your L/C yet; please take up the matter with the issuing bank at once.

(5) Much to our regret, we have not yet received your letter of credit against our Sales Confirmation No. 3246, although it should have reached us by the end of March, as stipulated, so please make sure that your L/C should reach us before . . .

3. Making amendment to L/C

(1) On examination of the L/C stipulations, we found the following {discrepancies / mistakes / points} do not conform to the terms contracted. Therefore, please instruct your bank to make the necessary amendments.

(2) You are requested to amend the covering L/C to read as follows:

(3) Please amend the L/C to read "This L/C will expire on August 20, 2015 in China."

(4) Please delete/insert the world "about" before the quantity in your L/C No. 123.

(5) You are requested to have the related credit that includes "Transshipment and partial

shipments are allowed."

(6) As direct steamers to your port are few and far between, we have to ship the goods via ... therefore, we hope that your L/C should be amended to read, "Transshipment is allowed."

4. Requesting extension of L/C

(1) Under the circumstances, we earnestly hope that you will extend the credit to the end of this month.

(2) We are sorry that owing to some delay on the part of our suppliers we are unable to get the goods ready before the end of this month, so we hope that you can extend the shipment date of your L/C to ... and validity to ... thus enabling us to effect shipment of goods in question.

(3) Due to uncontrollable factors, we cannot ship the goods as agreed, so we earnestly hope that you can
{
allow us further extension of the credit to the date of ...
give us ample time to negotiate the draft under the credit to the end of this month.
have your L/C extended before it expires.
}

(4) We are sorry that we cannot deliver the goods within the time as stipulated, due to some unexpected situation, we sincerely hope to see the L/C will be extended to the date of ...

I Put the following terms or phrases form English into Chinese or vice versa.

1. beneficiary
2. an irrevocable L/C
3. documentary L/C
4. sales confirmation
5. bill of lading
6. delivery date
7. 商业发票
8. 汇票
9. 保险单
10. 议付行
11. 催开信用证
12. 信用证延期

II Fill in the blanks of the following letters with the words given below, and change the form when necessary.

speed, complete, via, on , stock, issue, read, delay

Dear Mr. Gray,

Your letter of credit No. 8965 _____ by the Bank of Cyprus has arrived. _____ examination, we find that transshipment and partial shipment are not allowed.

As direct sailings to Limassol are infrequent, we have to ship _____ Rotterdam more often than not. As a result, transshipment may be necessary. With regard to partial shipment, it would _____ matters up if we could ship immediately the goods we have in _____ instead of waiting for the whole shipment to be _____.

With this in mind, I faxed you today, asking for the letter of credit to be amended to _____: "partial shipment and transshipment allowed".

I trust this amendment will meet with your approval and you will fax us to that effect without _____.

Yours sincerely,

III Translate the following sentences into English.

1. 我们的惯例是：接受保兑的、不可撤销的、有效期为装船后 3 周的即期信用证。
2. 请注意第 267 号合同项下的 600 辆自行车备妥待运已久，但至今我们尚未收到你方的有关信用证。请尽早开来，以便装运。
3. 我们很高兴地告知，以你方为受益人的金额为 35 000 美元的 MI1926 号信用证已由商业银行开出。
4. 根据 328 号合同的规定，有关信用证应不迟于 3 月 2 号到达我处，我们希望你能及时开出信用证，以避免装运延误。
5. 请把 985SD86 号信用证修改为"允许转运"。另因此笔交易是以 CFR 条款达成的，故请删除有关保险单的条款。
6. 由于供货商的延误，我们不能按信用证规定在 8 月 20 日之前发货，故请将信用证的船期和有效期分别延展一个月。
7. 非常遗憾，我们不得不拒绝贵方付款交单支付方式的请求，因为我们只接受即期信用证的支付方式。
8. 因此，在与国外客户的所有交易中，暂时歉难接受 D/A 条款。

IV Write a letter in English asking for amendment to the following letter of credit by checking it with the given contract terms.

1.

COMMERCIAL BANK OF THATTOWN
                         Date: Oct. 5, 2015
To: Shanghai Cereals, Oils & Foodstuffs Imp/Exp Corporation
    Shanghai, China
Advised through Bank of China, Shanghai
                         No. BOC 15/10/05
DOCUMENTARY LETTER OF CREDIT IRREVOCABLE

Dear Sirs:

You are authorised to draw on Hong Kong Food Company, Vancouver for a sum not exceeding CAN $120,000 (SAY CANADIAN DOLLARS ONE HUNDRED AND TWENTY THOUSAND ONLY) available by draft drawn on them at sight accompanied by the following documents:

(1) Full set of Clean on Board Bill of Lading made out to order and blank endorsed, marked "freight to collect" dated not later than November 30, 2015 and notify accountee.
(2) Signed Commercial Invoice in quintuplicate.
(3) Canadian Customs Invoice in quintuplicate.
(4) Insurance Policies (or Certificates) in duplicate covering Marine and War Risks.

Evidencing shipment from China port to Montreal, Canada of the following goods:
50,000 tins of 430 grams of Maling Brand Strawberry Jam, at CAN $2.50 per tin CFRC 3% Vancouver, details as per your S/C No. 06/8712.

Partial shipments are allowed.

This credit expires on November 30, 2015 for negotiation in China.

2.
合同主要条款如下：
卖方：上海粮油食品进出口公司
买方：温哥华香港食品公司
商品名称："梅林"牌草莓酱
规格：340克听装
数量：50 000听
单价：CFR温哥华每听2.5加元，含佣金3%
总值：125 000加元

装运期：2015年11月自中国港口运往温哥华，允许转船和分批装运

付款条件：凭不可撤销的即期信用证付款。信用证议付有效期应为最后装运期后第15天在中国到期。

合同号码：06/8712

V Writing practice.

Situational Writing 1

You have received an order of 200 computers amounting to US$12,000, and you are preparing to make shipment by the end of this month. But you have not received your L/C. So you will request your buyer to open an irrevocable L/C in your favor soon. **Please write a letter to ask for establishment of L/C so that you can ship the goods earlier and accordingly obtain the relevant documents.**

Situational Writing 2

You are an importer and are writing to your exporter, informing the company that you have just received an import license and you can increase your total amount of L/C No. NBB879 to USD160,000, you will send an L/C amendment advice to your exporter, telling him that you will make an amendment to the original letter to extend the shipment and validity dates of the L/C to November 16 and 30 respectively. **You are requested to write a letter in which you inform the exporter of the above-mentioned particulars.**

Unit 8

Other Methods of Payment
其他付款方式

8.1 Introduction of Other Methods of Payment

Payment is the most important and complicated part in business and settlement of foreign trade may be made in many ways, such as payment in advance, open account terms, consignment sales, etc. But the most often adopted methods of payment in international trade are as follows: collection, remittance and letter of credit. As for the letter of credit, it has been introduced in the previous unit, this unit will not discuss it. Before knowing the above methods of payment, please learn something about an important instrument in payment, i. e. draft.

8.1.1 Bill of Exchange

A bill of exchange or a draft is an unconditional written order drawn or issued by the drawer to the drawee or another person for certain amount of money to be paid to someone, or the ordered one, or the holder at sight, or at a fixed time in the future or at the time stated.

Payment in international trade is seldom made with cash, but mostly with the worldwide used instrument of bill of exchange, check and promissory, especially with draft in chief.[1] It has two forms: a sight draft and a usance draft (also called a time draft or a term draft).

8.1.2 Collection

It means the creditor (exporter) issues the bill of exchange and entrusts the bank to collect the payment of the shipment from the debtor (importer). Documentary collection falls into two major forms: Documents against Payment (D/P) and Documents against Acceptance (D/A).

8.1.3 Remittance

Remittance, like collection, is another mode of payment based on commercial credit. It means the buyer sends the payment through bank or other forms to the receiver initiatively. It is widely used for payment in advance, cash with order and open account business. It has three forms: mail transfer (M/T), telegraphic transfer (T/T) and demand draft (D/D).

Nowadays, there is a development of the introduction of a procedure known as "SWIFT" system (Society for Worldwide Inter-bank Financial Telecommunication) for passing and receiving international payment. The system is characterized by its uniform format, fast transfer and low costs.

8.2 Writing for Other Methods of Payment

It is often the case for customers to ask for other methods of payment in their transactions: payment extension, payment in installments, D/P at sight or D/A, cash in advance, etc. It is a hard job, because you need to try to make the receiver of your letter understand and accept your request, while you are keeping sensitive to maintain relations with your trade partners.

In presenting your request, you will have to provide your reasons or other convincing evidence to prove the merit of your request, including facts, figures, expert opinions, examples, and details. If it is possible, you can suggest direct and indirect benefits for the receiver. But at the same time announcement of your request should be clear but understated, trying to avoid anything blunt to damage the climate for your possibly successful request. If your request is very likely to be refused, you should identify what factors will be obstacles to the receiver and offer your arguments. But your tone should not sound emotional. Where it seems natural, you can include compliment or anything else to make the receiver feel better.

8.3 Letter Samples

Letter 8-1 (Asking for D/P)

Dear Sirs,

We thank you for your order No. 1368 and are pleased to inform you that the goods required have been dispatched by S. S. "Garden", due at Singapore on the 19th, August.^{2}

We are sure that you can understand our position that on this occasion it is necessary to make this a "Document against Payment" transaction, since we have not had time to secure credit references on your firm. We have drawn a sight draft on you for the amount of US$ 8,500 through the Merchant Bank Ltd. of Singapore, who will approach you in a few days for the payment of the draft. They will then hand to you the full documents to enable you to take delivery.

We hope that in due course we will be able to establish regular trading with you.[3] In such circumstances we would be prepared to give you a three-month credit once your references are secured. We hope that this will be only the first of many orders you will place with us.

Faithfully yours,

 Letter 8-2 (Buyer proposes payment by D/A)

Dear Sirs,

We wish to place with you a trial order for 150 cases of[4] Canned Luncheon Meat at your price of US$ 300 per case CFR Kuwait for shipment during October/November.

As this particular order involves a relatively small amount and we have only moderate means at hand, we would suggest payment by D/A at 60 days' sight. If the trial sale proves successful, you may count on us for further orders.

We hope you can give our proposal your most favorable consideration and await your early reply.

Truly yours,

 Letter 8-3 (Asking for easier payment terms)

Dear Sirs,

In the past, our purchases of steel pipes from you have normally been paid by confirmed, irrevocable letter of credit.

This arrangement has cost us a great deal of money. From the moment we open the credit until our buyers pay us normally, funds have been tied up for about four months.

This is currently a particularly serious problem for us in view of the difficult economic climate and the prevailing high interest rates.⁵

If you could offer us easier payment terms, it would probably lead to an increase in business between our companies. We propose either cash against documents on arrival of goods, or drawing on us at three month's sight.⁶

We hope our request will meet your agreement and look forward to your early reply.

Yours faithfully,

 Letter 8-4（Suggesting payment by D/P instead of D/A）

Dear Sirs,

We thank you for your letter of 24 this month, from which we have learnt that you suggest our accepting payment by D/A as you think it does not pay to open a L/C for a small order.

After taking your suggestion into due consideration, we think the best we can do at present is to agree to payment by D/P at 30 days' sight. And with the development of our business, we will consider more flexible ways to cooperate with you in the near future. The goods under your order have been ready for shipment and we will deliver them within the contracted time after receipt of your confirmation of payment terms.

We hope that you will find the shipment satisfactory to you and are looking forward to your regular orders.

Yours faithfully,

 Letter 8-5（Refusing payment by D/A）

Dear Sirs,

Thank you for your order of August 15 and we are pleased to learn that you intend to give our Canned Luncheon Meat a trial sale in your market.

While we appreciate your good intention, we regret being unable to accept your request for payment by D/A 60 days' sight. As we generally require payment by irrevocable letter of credit available by draft at sight, we cannot make any arrangement contrary to our usual practice, especially for a new customer. May we suggest that we do business on the basis of payment by L/C first and leave the matter to be discussed at a later date?

We hope the above payment terms are acceptable to you and look forward to your confirmation.

Yours faithfully,

 Letter 8-6（Payment by T/T）

Dear Sirs,

We have received your statement for the quarter that ended September 30 and found that it agrees with our books. As requested, we have instructed our bankers to send the sum of US$5,000 by T/T for the credit of your account of the Bank of China, Beijing Branch.[7]

This payment that clears your account up to August 31 the unpaid balance of US$2,000 for the goods supplied during September will be telegraphed by our bankers on or before November 15.

Yours faithfully,

 Letter 8-7（Asking for T/T payment）

Dear Sirs,

We have studied the specifications and price list of your new paints and varnishes and now wish to place the enclosed order with you.

As we are in urgent need of several of the items, we should be glad if you would make up and ship the order as soon as you possibly can.

In the past we dealt with you on sight credit basis. Now, we would like to propose a different way of payment, i. e. , when the goods purchased by us are ready for shipment and freight space booked, we will remit you the full amount by T/T. The reasons are that we can thus more confidently assure our buyers of the time of delivery and save a lot of expenses on opening the letter of credit.[8] As we feel this would not make much difference to you but would facilitate our sales, we hope you will grant our request.

We look forward to your confirmation of our order and your affirmative reply to our new arrangements of payment.

Yours faithfully,

Letter 8-8 (Asking for accepting the draft)

Dear Sirs,

As to this business, we will draw our draft at 30d/s on you against the 200 units of the construction machines for a sum amounting to US$150,000 under the L/C.

We ask you to accept it on presentation and honor it on maturity.[9]

Faithfully yours,

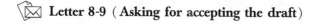

Letter 8-9 (Asking for accepting the draft)

Dear Sirs,

We thank you for your order of 25th July for 10,000 meters of poplin shirting at the quoted price of US$1.24 per meter.

The shirting is now ready for dispatch and will be shipped by the S. S. Tripoli sailing from Liverpool on 18th August.

We are pleased to enclose the shipping documents. Also enclosed is our sight draft drawn at 30 days as agreed. Please accept and return it immediately.

Yours faithfully,

Unit 8 Other Methods of Payment

 Letter 8-10（Asking to change the method of payment）

Dear Mr. Smith,

Thank you for being so prompt in sending the sales confirmation against our last order No. KK78901. We have established the covering L/C, and the bank should be sending you an advice in no time.[10]

We have been dealing with you on the L/C basis for over a year and would like to change to payment by 30-day bill of exchange, documents against payment.

When we first contacted you in March last year, you told us that you would be prepared to reconsider terms of payment once we had established a trading association. We think that sufficient time has elapsed for us to be allowed the terms we have asked for. If you need references, we will be glad to supply them.

As we will be sending another order within the month, could you please confirm that you agree to these terms of payment?

Attached is the Sales Confirmation No. 980654 we have countersigned and returned for your file.

Yours sincerely,

Words and Vocabulary

collection	n.	托收
remittance	n.	汇付，汇款
entrust	v.	委托
initiatively	ad.	开始，起初
blunt	a.	坦率的，鲁莽的
appreciate	v.	理解
irrevocable	a.	不可撤销的
varnish	n.	（人工或天然的）光泽
remit	v.	汇款

affirmative	a.	肯定的
honor	v.	遵守（诺言）
maturity	n.	（票据等的）到期
dispatch	v.	发运，运输
elapse	v.	（时光）流逝
file	n.	档案

payment in advance	预付款
open account	赊销
consignment sales	寄售
bill of exchange	汇票
mail transfer	信汇
telegraphic transfer	电汇
demand draft	即期汇票
payment extension	付款延期
payment in installments	分期付款
trial sales	试销
irrevocable letter of credit	不可撤销信用证
poplin shirting	府绸衬衫料子
trading association	贸易关系

Notes

1. Payment in international trade is seldom made with cash, but mostly with the worldwide used instrument of bill of exchange, check and promissory, especially with draft in chief. 在国际贸易中很少用现金来支付，在大多数情况下都采用支付工具来进行付款。这些支付工具包括：汇票、支票、本票，而主要还是使用汇票。
   本句中的"instrument"是"支付工具"的意思。

2. ... and are pleased to inform you that the goods required have been dispatched by S. S. "Garden", due at Singapore on the 19th, August.　……我们很高兴地通知你方，你方所需要的货物已由"Garden"号货轮运出，将于8月19日到达新加坡。
   本句中的"S. S."为"steam ship"的缩写，意思为"货轮"；"due at ..."是"预期到达"的意思。

3. We hope that in due course we will be able to establish regular trading with you.
   希望届时我们将能与你方建立正常的贸易联系。
   本句中的"in due course"意思为"到时，届时"。

Unit 8 Other Methods of Payment

4. We wish to place with you a trial order for 150 cases of...
   我们试订购150箱……
   本句中的"place with you a trail order"意为"向你试订购……"。请注意："向某人下订单应"写为"place an order with someone"，而不是"make an order with someone"。但是，在表示向某人发盘时，可以是"make an offer to someone"。

5. This is currently a particularly serious problem for us in view of the difficult economic climate and the prevailing high interest rates. 从目前不景气的经济环境和现有的高利率来看，这个问题对我们来说尤其严重。
   本句中的"in view of"意为"根据，从……来看"。

6. We propose either cash against documents on arrival of goods, or drawing on us at three month's sight. 我们建议：在货物到达时，凭单付款，或者向我们开立见票3个月付款的汇票。

7. As requested, we have instructed our bankers to send the sum of US$ 5,000 by T/T for the credit of your account of the Bank of China, Beijing Branch. 根据你方要求，我们已经指示银行电汇给你方在中国银行北京分行账户5,000美元。
   本句中的"T/T"为"telegraphic transfer"的缩写，意为"电汇"。

8. The reasons are that we can thus more confidently assure our buyers of the time of delivery and save a lot of expenses on opening the letter of credit. 其原因是，我们能更为放心地使我们的客户确知货物的发运时间，同时可节省因开立信用证所产生的大量费用。
   本句中的"assure of..."意为"使某人确信，使某人放心"。

9. We ask you to accept it on presentation and honor it on maturity. 我们要求你方在我们提示汇票时加以承兑，并届时予以付款。
   本句中的"accept"为"承兑汇票"的意思，而"honor it on maturity"中的"honor"意为"履行承诺"，"on maturity"是指"汇票到期"。

10. We have established the covering L/C, and the bank should be sending you an advice in no time. 我们已开立了相关信用证，银行应会及时地通知你们。
    本句中的"establish the covering credit L/C"意为"开立相关信用证"，其中的"establish"为"开立（信用证）"的意思，"covering"等同于英文中的"relevant"。

Sentence Menu

1. Terms of payment

(1) Considering the small amount involved, we are prepared, as an exception, to accept payment by D/P at sight for the value of your first trial order.

(2) As a special accommodation, we agree to your proposal and accept payment by D/P at sight, but this should not be considered as a precedent.

(3) We understand that you are having some difficulty in opening L/C. Such being the case, we suggest D/P payment.

(4) With regard to terms of payment, we regret being unable to accept documents against payment.

(5) For a few special import items we can adopt "payment by installments".

(6) We will draw on you by our documentary draft at sight, on collection basis, without L/C.

(7) We are willing to draw on you, at 30 days' sight, documents against acceptance (D/A).

(8) In view of the small amount of this transaction, we agree to draw on you documentary sight draft.

(9) It will interest you to know that as a special sign of encouragement, we shall consider accepting payment by D/P during this sales-pushing stage.

(10) In order to facilitate your efforts in introducing our products to your market, we are now giving you a special accommodation by granting D/P.

(11) At your repeated request, we would grant you such favorable terms of payment as D/A 40 days after sight.

(12) For your shipment, we agree to draw on you at 60 days' sight, but this cannot be taken as a precedent.

(13) We regret to inform you that we have to decline your request for D/P terms as we only accept payment by L/C at sight.

(14) Since the amount involved is small, we are prepared, as an exception, to accept payment by D/A.

(15) In compliance with your request, we exceptionally accept delivery against D/P at sight, but this should not be regarded as a precedent.

(16) The usual 3% discount may be deducted if payment is made within 30 days on receipt of this statement.

(17) We were pleased to receive your bank check for US$ ... It has been credited to your account, which is now completely clear.

(18) We enclose our bank check for US$ 1,520 in settlement of your invoice No. 193.

(19) Under this installment plan, 15% of the contract value is to be paid with order.

2. Request for payment

(1) It has been our usual practice to do business with payment by D/P at sight instead of by L/C. We should, therefore, like you to accept D/P terms for this transaction and future ones.

(2) Please remit the 10% down payment to us by T/T. Payment of balance is to be made in three installments.

(3) It is expensive to open an L/C and tie up the capital of a small company like ours, so it is better for us to adopt D/P or D/A.

(4) It should be pointed out that the contract value in Malaysian dollars will be converted into Hong Kong dollars in payment at the conversion rate then prevailing.

(5) Please surrender these documents to the drawee against their accepting the draft and

$$\begin{cases} \text{collect and remit the net proceeds to us.} \\ \text{give the draft their protection.} \\ \text{give our draft their due honor.} \end{cases}$$

Exercises

I Put the following terms or phrases from English into Chinese or vice versa.

1. D/A
2. remittance
3. time draft
4. D/P after sight
5. documentary collection
6. balance
7. 电汇
8. 预付现金
9. 承兑交单
10. 分期付款
11. 不可撤销信用证
12. 汇票

II Fill in the blanks of the following letters with the words given below, and change the form when necessary.

on, standing, enquiry, place, trial, therefore, prospect

Dear Sirs,

We are the largest wholesaler in Kuwait and have recently received a number of _____ for your stainless steal cutlery. We think there are good _____ for the sale of this cutlery, but at present it is little known here and as we cannot count _____ regular sales we do not feel able to make purchases on our own account.

We are, _____, writing to suggest that you send us a _____ delivery for sale on D/A terms. We make the proposal hoping to _____ firm orders when the market is established.

We believe our proposal offers good prospects and hope you will be willing to give it a trial. As to our _____, you may check it with our bankers, the National Bank of Kuwait.

Yours faithfully,

III Compare the following two letters and point out why the revision is made so.

The original letter

Dear Sir or Madam:

With reference to your due commission, our records show that a money order in the amount of US$ 166.83 was indeed sent to the following address:

> Mid-West Travel Service, Inc.
> Evanston Illinois Branch
> 225 Church Street
> Evanston, Illinois 60201
> USA

Please find copies of the statements and money order enclosed. If you have any questions, we suggest for you to direct further inquiries to the Bank of Asia.

At this point we wish to ask you a question regarding the above matter. Shall we send our commission checks to the branch office that makes the reservation, or shall we send it directly to your home office? We would appreciate it if you would let us know as soon as possible so we can prevent this occurrence in the future.

We await your reply.

Faithfully yours,

John Mak
Manager

The revised letter

Dear Sirs,

Thank you for your message of April 30 inquiring about the commission due.

Our records show that a money order for US$ 166.83 was sent to the following office:

> Mid-West Travel Service, Inc.
> Evanston Illinois Branch
> 225 Church Street
> Evanston, Illinois 60201
> USA

Enclosed are copies of the statements and money order.

To avoid future problems, would you please let us know if we should send our commission check(s) directly to the branch office that makes the reservation, or to your home office?

Faithfully yours,

John Mak
Manager

IV Translate the following passages into English.

敬启者：

  你方3月10号的来函收悉。我方已认真考虑过你方以 D/A 方式试销我方餐刀之建议。兹奉告，以试销方式促进交易，我方能破例做到的只能按即期 D/P 条件办理。

  因我方餐刀以质量上乘、设计新颖、价格合理而著称，所以接受我方建议，你们不会承担任何风险。此种餐刀正畅销许多国家。我们相信，在你方店里也一定会畅销。

  如对我方建议感兴趣，请复函，我方将再次同你方联系。

敬上

V Writing practice.

Situational Writing 1

Write an English letter by making use of the ideas given below.

- 我方一直以保兑的、不可撤销的信用证支付从贵处购买产品。
- 但是，此种支付方式对我方来说费用高，资金占用时间长，银行利息高。
- 建议采用"即期付款交单"或"见票后30天付款"。

Situational Writing 2

You have already shipped the goods and passed on your shipping documents including bill of lading, invoice, and insurance, etc, as well as a draft to the remitting bank for collection. **You are now requested to write a letter to inform the importer of the above mentioned particulars and ask the company to pay the draft 30 days after sight.**

Unit 9

Collection Letters
催 款 函

9.1 Introduction

Business companies must collect the receivables or the money for the products or services they sell on credit. Most buyers honor their agreement to pay. In reality, however, some buyers postpone or evade payment for various reasons. Some may forget; some may put off their payment; some may have been trapped in financial problems and cannot afford to pay; and a few never intend to pay. Under such circumstances, the sellers will have to send collection letters for the money that is due or overdue.

9.1.1 Collection Appeals

As in other persuasive message, the primary purpose of a collection letter is to get action (payment). A secondary goal is to maintain a customer's goodwill and therefore collection letters are a special form of persuasive writing. In the following we will discuss some of the elements of persuasion that usually determine the effectiveness of a collection letter.

1. **Short and written inductively**

Collection letters are generally written inductively; but they are shorter than other letters. Normally, customers know that they owe (no need to devote space to informing them) and they expect to be asked for payment, so there is no need to get attention of the receiver, nor is there an apology. If a letter is short, its main point stands out vividly. Compared with a long letter, a short letter has a greater chance of being read in its entirety. In a long letter, the main point might be in the skipped-over portion or may have to compete for attention with minor points. [1]

2. **Avoidance of emotional appeal**

People are influenced by emotions. Prior to the mild-appeal stage of the collection series, the use of emotional appeal should be minimal and subtle. The writer should adopt a businesslike, firm, yet friendly and considerate tone. Beginning with the mild-appeal stage, though, the writer can attempt to engage the reader's emotions more seriously.

3. Use of a credible, sincere image

The main principle is that we have already sent the purchaser the goods he required and, in return, as a buyer, he or she should pay for the benefits he has received. What we ask for is just something in exchange. It is a fair treatment. Therefore, writer must appear determined to collect what is due, yet unthreatening and, at least in the early collection stages, willing to adapt to the readers' reasonable consideration.

4. Avoidance of disrupting the reader's expectations

A debtor knows for sure that the creditor will ask for payment, and therefore they are very sensitive about the respect especially at the early time, and like anyone else, they also expects to be treated like a human being. Be sure not to let your reader lose "face".

5. Careful choice of words

Wording may vary with collection series. Early stages in the collection series call for words that can create pleasant, cooperative feelings such as *appreciate, cooperation* and so on. In mid-stage, words like legal remedies, forced to take steps can be used to create more serious, and perhaps more motivating feelings if necessary. Only in the final stage can the writer select the words that emphasize the negative orientation to cause considerable uneasiness.

The following are some of the typical phrases or sentences used at different times.

(1) Early stage:

Become due

Have not yet received your payment

May we remind you ...

May we hear from you about non-delivery or payment, please?

(2) Mid-stage:

Be forced to take steps

Unless payment is received by the date ...

Please send us your cheque without further delay.

(3) Final stage:

Hand the case to our lawyers

The matter will be placed in the hands of our lawyers.

9.1.2 Collection Series

Knowing that slow-to-pay customers may not respond to the first attempt at collection, businesses that use collection letters normally use a series (if the first letter does not bring a response, a second letter is sent, then a third, and so on). The procedure in a collection series is one of increasing forcefulness. The stages are as follows:

1. Reminder

Many people will pay promptly when they receive a bill. Shortly after the due date, simple reminder will usually bring in most of the remaining accounts. The reminder is typically a duplicate of the original statement with rubber-stamped notation saying "second notice", "past due", or "please remit". To send a collection letter at this stage would be risky for goodwill. The assumption is that the obligation has been overlooked and will be paid when the reminder is received. Very often, companies will use two or three reminders before moving to the letter-writing stage. They should be used only when a company is reasonably sure collection is going to be difficult.

2. Inquiry

After sending the normal number of reminders without success, companies resort to letters. To increase efficiency, many organizations use form letters that may be initiated automatically by the computer or by a collector.[2] In either case, the form letters are personalized by inserting the debtor's name and address, salutation, amount owed, and date payment is due. In all letters at the inquiry stage, the assumption must be that something has prevented the debtor from paying. The aim is to get some action from the customer in the form of either a check or an explanation. The writer should be empathic, writing and thinking positively. Therefore the tone of the letter should be direct, consultative, and polite, making it easy for the debtor to reply, but not providing the debtor with any excuses for non-payment. Unlike the reminders, the letter of inquiry here is only once delivered.

3. Urgency

If the debtor still remains silent after the inquiry is made, a letter of mild appeal should be sent. In order to persuade the debtor to pay the bill, the writer should make appropriate and increasingly forceful appeals. If there is still no response from the debtor after a mild appeal has been sent out for a quite some time, a letter of urgency should be sent. The tone at this moment is insistent, firm, and direct, but still remains a chance for the debtor to get through.[3]

4. Ultimatum

When a letter of urgency fails to do its work, the collection writer must take the only remaining course of action: a letter that says, "You must pay now of your own volition or we will use every possible legal means to enforce collection." The debtor must pay or face the consequences. Whatever recourse you will have to use for final collection must be mentioned in the letter. You must make the most of the fact that you will use the courts, a collection agency, or an attorney to enforce collection. Unfortunately, accounts that have reached this stage may be costly to the lender as they are to the borrower.

At this stage, your letter should not use language that will make you susceptible to legal action by the customer. You need to keep your self-control, and show some patience to stay above the name-calling level. Any effort you can make to retain goodwill is worthwhile. Above all, avoid preaching because debtors who get to this stage do not react favorably to advice about how they should have acted.[4]

Note that writing of ultimatum is structured deductively at this late stage. The letter could emphasize the ultimatum at the beginning of the letter to tell the debtor that you are taking the steps promised. The account is no longer in your hands.

9.2 Letter Samples

 Letter 9-1（The reminder of overdue payment）

Dear Sirs,

We have not received your payment for Order No. 625, which was due on Oct. 16, 2015.

It would be appreciated if you could have it remitted to us by Oct. 30, 2015.

Yours faithfully,

 Letter 9-2（The reminder of overdue payment）

Dear Sirs,

Have you overlooked the unpaid balance from your recent purchase? If your payment is already on the way to us, please accept our thanks. Otherwise, won't you check and mail the remittance right now?

Thank you for cooperation.

Yours truly,

 Letter 9-3（The inquiry for overdue payment）

Dear Sirs,

Account No. 8675

According to our closing accounts for the first quarter of the year, our account for the paint and wallpaper supplied to you on 16 March has not yet been settled.[5]

We enclose a detailed statement, which shows the amount owing to be RMB yuan 68,000, and hope you will be able to make an early settlement.

Yours faithfully,

 Letter 9-4（**The inquiry for overdue payment**）

Dear Sir or Madam:

We have not heard from you for the past two months.

Your Order No. 687 for the printers is still unpaid, which is past due. We believe something special has prevented you from continuing your prompt paying practice.

Will you please either remit the unpaid balance of US$6,000 to cover the overdue payment or give us your plan for meeting your obligation?

We are looking forward to your reply.

Faithfully yours,

 Letter 9-5（**Urgent appeal for overdue payment**）

Dear Sir or Madam:

I have recently sent you a letter regarding the outstanding balance of your account with this shop. According to our records, you have failed to make any repayments whatsoever and the sum of HK$5000 is now overdue.

We understand that it is sometimes difficult to meet our debts. We are therefore prepared to overlook the fact that you have missed the first three repayments if you undertake to meet the repayments schedule from now on.[6]

Also, if you would like to extend the period of credit so that repayments are made easier, we should be happy to discuss the matter with you.

Unit 9   Collection Letters

We certainly would not like to reduce your credit limit for future purchases. I urge you in the strongest terms, therefore, to contact me within the next seven days so that this unfortunate situation can be sorted out.

I look forward to hearing from you within the next week.

Yours truely,

 Letter 9-6 (Urgent appeal for overdue payment)

Dear Mr. Smith,

How much is it worth to you? It is your credit record I am referring to, and it's a most important question to you, now that it hangs in the balance.

The good reference we were given on you when you opened your account told us that you have successfully handled your promises to pay promptly for a long time.[7] We know that you must want to maintain this good rating, for it means so much to you. Aside from the obvious advantages of credit buying, it is important to your CI.[8] The business would judge you by how you fulfill your promises.

Because your credit record means so much to you, it is hard to understand how you have permitted your account of US$ 8,000 to run six months past due. Save your good.

Send us your payment today.

Yours sincerely,

 Letter 9-7 (Ultimatum)

Dear Mr. Alexander,

When we agreed some three months ago to ship medical supplies and equipment, you agreed that you would pay US$ 6,000 within 30 days. Yet the 30 days have gone by, then 60. Now more than 90 days have elapsed.

117

Because our overdue notices and letters have gone unanswered, our patience is exhausted; however, our interest in you and in your welfare is not. Your name will be submitted as "non-pay" unless we receive your check for US$6,000 by July 29. The effect of a bad report could restrict your ability to purchase medical supplies and equipment on credit. In addition, our legal department would be forced to bring suit for collection.

We have every right to enforce legal collection. You have until July 29 to retain your good record and to avoid legal embarrassment.[9]

Sincerely yours,

 Letter 9-8 (Ultimatum)

Dear Mr. Wilson,

Is there any reason you have not paid your bill of US$3,680?

In the credit agreement you signed, you agreed to pay off your bill in three payments. Your total bill is now overdue. Please send US$3,680 within 10 days. If you have any questions or concerns regarding this bill, please contact me at 800-666-9765 by October 21, 2015.

Failure to send the full amount by October 21 may mean that your bill is turned over to a collection agency. Your prompt attention is urgent to protect your credit.

Sincerely yours,

Mary West
Credit Manager

 Letter 9-9 (Ultimatum)

Dear Mr. Johnson,

Subject: Overdue Loan Repayments (Account No. 067809)

I refer to my letter of 17th August regarding your failure to meet your loan repayments.

According to my records, repayments totaling US＄20,000 are currently overdue. This represents repayments for the last three months.

I spoke to your assistant on the telephone today and he informed me that you had no intention of repaying the money owed to us. I should remind you that the US＄300,000 you borrowed from the Third Bank of Chicago was used to expand your premises, and that it has led to increased profits on your part. We do not, therefore, feel it unfair to expect you to honor our agreement.

I have written to you several times asking you to contact me to discuss the matter so that we might come to an arrangement. However, on all occasions, you have ignored my letters.

It is regretful that I must inform you that unless we receive full payment within the next three days. I shall be compelled to instruct our legal department to begin proceedings against you.[10]

Yours sincerely,

Mr. Peter Lusardi
Overdue Accounts Division

Words and Vocabulary

receivables	n.	（复数）应收款项
evade	v.	逃避，避开
overdue	a.	逾期的
inductively	ad.	（指逻辑学、数学上）归纳地
skipped-over	a.	跨越的，越过的
subtle	a.	难以描述的，细微的
disrupting	a.	有破坏性的
creditor	n.	债权人
orientation	n.	倾向
duplicate	n.	复印件
rubber-stamped	a.	盖了图章的

initiate	v.	开始实施，发起
personalize	v.	使个性化
insert	v.	插入，加入
emphatic	a.	强调的，加强语气的
consultative	a.	协商的，商量的
appeal	n.	诉求
insistent	a.	坚持的
ultimatum	n.	最后通牒
volition	n.	意愿
recourse	n.	求助的对象
attorney	n.	律师
susceptible	a.	易受影响或损害的
name-calling	a.	骂人的，侮辱人的
favorably	ad.	肯定地，赞成地
deductively	ad.	演绎地
balance	n.	剩余款
obligation	n.	义务
outstanding	a.	剩余的
repayment	n.	偿付，偿还
notice	n.	通知
suit	n.	诉讼
embarrassment	n.	尴尬
compelled	a.	被迫的
instruct	v.	指示，指令
proceedings	n.	诉讼程序

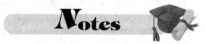

Notes

1. In a long letter, the main point might be in the skipped-over portion or may have to compete for attention with minor points. 在长信中，主要观点很可能会出现在容易被读者忽略的段落中，与那些不太重要的观点出现在一起，等待读者的关注。
   本句中的"skipped over"为"跳读过去"的意思。

2. To increase efficiency, many organizations use form letters that may be initiated automatically by the computer or by a collector. 为了提高工作效率，许多组织使用格式信件，由计算机自动生成，或由催款人打印出来。
   本句中的"form letter"是指"格式信件"或"事先打印好的信件"。

3. The tone at this moment is insistent, firm, and direct, but still remains a chance for the debtor to get through.　　在此阶段的语气应该是坚持原则，坚定不移，直截了当，但仍给债务人履行付款义务的机会。

本句中的"get through"是"继续履行付款义务"的意思。

4. Above all, avoid preaching because debtors who get to this stage do not react favorably to advice about how they should have acted.　　最为重要的是，应避免说教，因为债务人在这个阶段对任何建议都不会积极回应的。

5. According to our closing accounts for the first quarter of the year, our account for the paint and wallpaper supplied to you on 16 March has not yet been settled.　　我们本年度第一季节结束的财务报告显示，我们在3月16日销售给贵方的油漆和墙纸尚未结款。

6. We are therefore prepared to overlook the fact that you have missed the first three repayments if you undertake to meet the repayments schedule from now on.　　因此，如果贵方承诺从现在起支付货款，我们将不追究以前三次未能按期付款的事实。

7. ... you have successfully handled your promises to pay promptly for a long time.

……长期以来，贵方一直成功地恪守承诺，及时付款。

本句中的"successfully handled your promise"表明，信的作者暗示："有时没有遵守承诺是有客观原因的，并非故意行为"，作者这么写，实际上仍给对方足够的面子，以便进一步履行付款义务。

8. Aside from the obvious advantages of credit buying, it is important to your CI.　　凭信用购买产品不仅能给你带来很大的优势，而且对你们公司形象也是至关重要的。

本句中"CI"为"company image"的缩写。

9. We have every right to enforce legal collection. You have until July 29 to retain your good record and to avoid legal embarrassment.　　我们有权采取法律手段来索款，直至7月29日之前你们仍可保持良好的信用记录，并不会惹上官司。

10. I shall be compelled to instruct our legal department to begin proceedings against you.　　我们不得不指示我们的法律部门来起诉你们公司。

本句中的"proceedings against you"为"对你们提起诉讼"的意思。

Sentence Menu

1. Reminder

(1) Perhaps you have forgotten to send us your last order payment of US$ ... which is past due now. It would be appreciated if you could have it remitted to us by July 16.

(2) May we remind you that the payment of this invoice is now past due? A cheque of US$ ... by return of post would be appreciated.

(3) We would appreciate payment immediately so that your account can be brought up to date.

(4) Our records show that your January account for US$ ... is still unpaid. Would you please

send us your check or make payment as soon as you can?

(5) Have you forgotten to send us your last order payment, which was past due now. If you have not mailed it to us, please do so right away after you receive this letter.

2. Inquiries for overdue payments

(1) Since you have always paid promptly, we assume that some unusual circumstance has prevented a reply. We would appreciate your remittance by the end of this month so that we could record it and forward it to our Accounting Department with an explanation.

(2) Have you overlooked the unpaid balance from your recent purchase? We shall be greatly obliged if you will remit us a cheque of US$ …

(3) We would ask again that you promptly pay your outstanding account or, if you are unable to do so for any reason, you can contact us so that we may discuss the matter.

(4) Please accept this letter as a friendly request for payment without further delay so that we can continue to give you our full service.

3. Urgency for overdue payments

(1) For regular customers such as you, our terms of payment are most favorable. If you are good enough to settle this account promptly, there will be no necessity for us to alter the terms to your disadvantage.

(2) Our patience is exhausted. Unless we receive the overdue payment by July 30, we will have to take necessary steps. The choice you are going to make right now is extremely important to your business.

(3) I certainly would not like to reduce your credit limit for future purchases, not to contact a collection agency, which I shall be forced to do if we do not receive payment in the very near future.

(4) Unless you can settle the balance of US$ … our business cannot go ahead.

(5) We would like you to contact us immediately so that we may work out a specific arrangement and save your reputation by settling the outstanding account soon.

4. Ultimatum for overdue payments

(1) We regret we shall have no alternative but to …

(2) I greatly regret that I shall be obliged to …

(3) Unfortunately, I shall be compelled to …

(4) Regrettably I shall have no choice but to …

(5) If you are unable to settle your account by the end of next week, I am afraid we will be forced to pass the matter over to our legal department.

(6) If we do not receive the total overdue account of US$ … by October 22, we will have to ask our attorneys to collect it through court proceedings.

(7) We would prefer not to take any legal action against you, but we all have no choice unless you do what we request you to do above.

(8) Like you, we prefer to avoid any legal embarrassment, but you would leave us with no choice unless you send your remittance of US$ ... by December 30.

(9) Would you please settle this account within the next 10 days? Otherwise we shall have to hand this matter to our solicitors/refer this matter to our collection agency/seek legal action.

I Put the following terms or phrases from English into Chinese or vice versa.

1. invoice
2. overdue payment
3. outstanding balance
4. bill
5. repayment
6. legal collection
7. 信用度
8. 结账
9. 支票
10. 诉诸法律
11. 公司形象
12. 履约

II Fill in the blanks of the following letters with the words given below, and change the form when necessary.

Letter A

clear, reminder, stand, agree, on, receipt,

Dear Mr. Smith,

Thank you for your order No. 7342 of 29 January for 20 dozen ladies' skirts.

We would like to continue to serve you _____ open account terms, but to do this, your bills must be paid within 30 days as _____. Your balance on account No. 6784 is long overdue and _____ at US$ 3,000. This is a second _____ so please send payment on _____ of this letter

Immediately, the overdue sum is _____, we will fulfill your current order.

Thank you for your cooperation.

Yours faithfully,

Letter B

> overlook, miss, whatsoever, outstanding, extend, repossession, relate, meet

Dear Mr. Chen,

You recently received a statement of account showing credit repayment _____ to your purchase of YOYTA from Anglo Motors in October. According to our records you have failed to make any repayments _____ and the sum of £7,200 is now overdue.

We understand that it is sometimes difficult to _____ debts, especially at this very expensive time of year. So we are prepared to _____ the fact that you have _____ the first two repayments if you undertake to meet the repayment schedule from now on.

Also, if you would like to _____ the period of credit so that repayments are made easier, we should be happy to discuss the matter with you.

However, if we do not hear from you within the next seven days, I am afraid we shall be forced to consider passing the matter over to our legal department for _____ of the car and collection of the _____ sum.

I look forward to hearing from you within the next week.

Yours sincerely,

Ⅲ **The following sentences are not appropriately written in the letters of collections. Please revise them in the way that can well suit the tone and style in collections.**

1. After the telephone conversation we conducted this afternoon, I checked our records …
2. You still owed us US$ …
3. We look forward to the honor of receiving a remittance from your esteemed selves at your earliest convenience.
4. Should you not pay up soon, we would like to get our lawyers onto you.

Ⅳ **Translate the following letter of collection into English.**

敬启者：

我方已多次催促你方尽快处理欠款一事，但是到目前为止我们没有收到你方任何关于这一问题的消息，我们不得不再一次地提醒你方尽早处理这笔欠款。

我们不清楚你方不能按商定时间结清账款的原因,但是请你们严格按合同的约定履行付款义务。

除非我们能在一周内收到你方的答复,否则我们将提起诉讼。我们相信大家都不愿意看到你方信用受损,我们也无须走到这一步。

如你方已付款,敬请忘记这封信。敬候你方早日回复。

真诚地

V Writing practice.

Situational Writing

You are now a manager of a Beijing-based company, and you have not received the payment for one consignment of cotton shirts, which was exported to a company in Singapore about 5 months ago. During the time of which, you wrote 3 reminders and 2 letters, requesting the company to settle the account immediately, but you only got one letter from the importer in which some excuses were given to refuse to honor the payment. **This time you are going to write a letter of ultimatum to ask for payment this week.**

Unit 10

Packing
包　装

10.1 Introduction

Packing is of particular importance in foreign trade because goods have to travel long distance before reaching their destination — often across oceans or across continents. Accidents, rough weather, unloading and reloading on the way, everything has to be taken into consideration.

As the buyer has the right to expect that his goods will reach him in perfect condition, the seller has to get them into a nice, compact shape that will stay that way even during the roughest journey.

Packing must be strictly marked. Conveniently, outer packing marks mainly include transport marks, directive marks and warning marks. The transport marks consist of:

(1) consignor's or consignee's code name,
(2) number of the contract or the L/C,
(3) the port of destination,
(4) numbers of the packed goods,

and sometimes weight and dimensions, all of which can greatly facilitate identification and transportation. Take for example, directive marks are eye-catching figures and concise instructions concerning manner of proper handling, storing, loading and unloading of the packed goods like "USE NO HOOKS, THIS SIDE UP, KEEP DRY", etc. Warning marks are obvious symbols or words to warn people against the hidden danger of inflammation, explosives and poisonous products.

Packing usually varies with the nature of the contents. The most commonly used packing containers are cartons, cases, crates, drums, barrels, bales, tins, and carboys.

Details such as manner of packing, kinds of packing materials and the burden of packing cost should be unmistakably stipulated in the contract concerned and strictly observed by both the selling side and the buying side.[1]

Letters about packing issues should be concise and clear. In such letters, the seller can describe in detail to the buyer his customary packing of the goods concerned and also indicate clearly that he may accept any required packing at the expense of the buyer. The buyer can inform the seller of any formerly unexpected requirements or fears about the packing. Any changes regarding packing stipulated in the contract should be mutually discussed and determined before shipment.

10.2 Letter Samples

 Letter 10-1（Packing instruction）

Dear Sir or Madam:

We enclose the countersigned copy of contract No. 350 of the 4th May 2015 for 350 bales of printed cottons. The letter of credit is on its way to you.

Please mark the bales with our initials, with the destination and contract number as follows:

KT
LONDON
250

This will apply to all shipments unless otherwise instructed.

Please advise us by fax as soon as shipment is effected.

Yours faithfully,

 Letter 10-2（Packing instruction）

Dear Sirs,

Thank you for your quotation of March 23 and the sample sweaters sent to us recently. We find both the price and quality satisfactory and herewith enclose our order form for 300 dozen each of men's and women's woolen sweaters at the prices stated in your quotation.

As this is our first order, we would like to state our detailed packing requirements. We want the sweaters to be packed each in a polybag, 6 dozen to a carton lined with waterproof paper.[2] If the cartons are not strong enough, most of them will be liable to go broken on arrival. So we would require that the carton be bound with double iron straps outside.[3]

We hope these packing requirements can be met and await your early shipment.

Yours faithfully,

Letter 10-3(**Packing instruction**)

Dear Sirs,

Please pack the captioned machines in a strong wooden case and wrap and pad generously all polished parts of the machine to avoid scratches and knocks against the container.

Also please put the machine in a case of about 12 cubic meters covered with waterproof cloth and strapped vertically and horizontally with metal bands and cut ventholes in the case to minimize condensation.[4]

Thank you for your sincere cooperation.

Yours faithfully,

 Letter 10-4(**Negotiation over shipping marks**)

Dear Sirs,

<u>Sales Confirmation NO. 89A/56</u>

We thank you for your letter of October 12, 2015, enclosing the above Sales Contract in duplicate but wish to state that the packing clause in the contract is not clear enough. The relative clause should read:

Packing: Seaworthy export packing, suitable for long distance ocean transportation.

The shirts under the captioned contract should be packed in plastic bags, five dozen to one carton, 20 cartons on a pallet, and 10 pallets in FCL container.[5] On the outer packing please mark our initials: JHCL in a triangle, under which the port of destination and our order number should be stenciled. In addition, directive marks like WATERPROOF, etc. should also be indicated.

We have made a footnote on the contract to that effect and are returning herein one copy of the contract, duly countersigned by us. We hope you will find it in order and pay special attention to the packing.

We look forward to receiving your shipping advice soon and thank you in advance.

Faithfully yours,

Letter 10-5（Packing and shipping marks instructions）

Dear Sirs,

We thank you for your packing instruction, but regret our inability to comply with your request for special packing.

In order to finalize this initial trade activity between us, we would like to make the following suggestions for your consideration.

1. The bed spreads will be packed 6 dozen to a packet, 4 packets to a carton and 8 cartons to a crate.
2. Your initials will be printed in a diamond instead of the full name.
3. The name of the country of origin of the goods will be marked on the carton and crate, not on every packet.
4. Special directions and warnings will be stenciled on the crate, not on every carton.

Please inform us your comments by return fax.

Yours truly,

 Letter 10-6（Packing instruction）

Dear Sirs,

We regret to inform you that the 145 cartons of iron nails you shipped to Dubai on May 12, 2015 were badly damaged, which is of course not your fault.

We are now writing to you about the packing of these nails, which we think necessary to clarify for our future dealings.

The packing for Dubai is to be in wooden cases of 112 lbs net, each containing 7 lbs ×16 packets.⁶ For Malta, we would like to have the goods packed in double gunny bags of 50-60 kilos each. As for the British market, our buyers prefer 25-kilo cartons.

Would you please tell us whether these requirements could be met?

Yours faithfully,

Letter 10-7（Suggestion for carton packing）

Dear Sirs,

Please be informed that for your future orders we shall pack our garments in cartons instead of in wooden cases, as packed in cartons has the following advantages.

1. It will prevent skillful pilferage as the traces of pilferage will be more in evidence.
2. It is fairly fit for ocean transportation.
3. Our cartons are well protected against moisture by plastic lining.
4. Cartons are comparatively light and compact, so they are more convenient to handle.

Our comments above come from a comparative study of the characteristics of the two modes of packing, i.e. carton packing and wooden case packing, as well as the results of shipments already made. We hope you will accept our carton packing and assure you of our sincere cooperation.

Yours faithfully,

 Letter 10-8（Suggestion for improvement of packing）

Dear Sir or Madam:

We regret to inform you that of the 160 cartons of machine parts delivered to us last week, 2 were found broken and some of the contents were badly damaged clearly through improper packing.

In view of our long-standing business relations, we would not lodge a claim against you for the loss this time. But we feel it necessary to stress the importance of seaworthy packing for our future dealings.

Usually valves and all delicate machine parts should be wrapped in soft material packed in cardboard boxes. These in turn are to be packed in wooden cases in such a manner that movement inside the cases is impossible. Besides, rope and metal handle should be fixed to the cases to facilitate consignment.[7]

We look forward to your comments on the above.

Yours faithfully,

Unit 10 Packing

Words and Vocabulary

destination	n.	目的地
compact	a.	紧密的，紧凑的
consignor	n.	发货人
consignee	n.	收货人
inflammation	n.	燃烧，易燃
carton	n.	纸板箱
crate	n.	木板箱
barrel	n.	木桶
carboy	n.	大玻璃瓶
vertically	ad.	竖向地
horizontally	ad.	横向地
venthole	n.	通风口
pallet	n.	（搬运货物用的）货盘
stencil	v.	刷唛头
diamond	n.	菱形
clarify	v.	澄清，讲清楚
pilferage	n.	偷窃
lining	n.	（衣服、箱子等的）内衬
seaworthy	a.	适航的
valve	n.	阀门
cardboard	n.	硬纸板
consignment	n.	一批货
iron strap		铁带，铁皮条
FCL container		整箱货柜
bed spread		床单
gunny bag		麻袋
lodge a claim against somebody		向某人起诉

Notes

1. Details such as manner of packing, kinds of packing materials and the burden of packing cost

should be unmistakably stipulated in the contract concerned and strictly observed by both the selling side and the buying side. 在相关的合同中应明确规定这样一些内容：包装方式、包装材料的类型、包装费用，同时，买卖双方应严格履行合同中的规定。

2. We want the sweaters to be packed each in a polybag, 6 dozen to a carton lined with waterproof paper. 我们要求每件毛线衫都装上塑料袋，6打装在一个内衬有防水纸的硬纸箱内。
   本句中的"lined with..."是"内衬有……"的意思。

3. So we would require that the carton be bound with double iron straps outside.
   因此，我们要求硬纸箱外面再用双道的金属条加固。

4. ...and strapped vertically and horizontally with metal bands and cut ventholes in the case to minimize condensation. 然后用铁条横向和纵向地予以加固，并在箱子上切一个通风孔以降低箱内的空气密度。

5. The shirts under the captioned contract should be packed in plastic bags, five dozen to one carton, 20 cartons on a pallet, and 10 pallets in FCL container. 该合同项下的衬衫必须装在塑料袋内，5打装一纸箱，20纸箱装一货盘，10货盘装一集装箱货柜。

6. The packing for Dubai is to be in wooden cases of 112 lbs net, each containing 7 lbs × 16 packets. 运往迪拜的货物应装在净重112英镑的木箱内，每只木箱内包含16个每个7英镑的货物包装箱。
   本句中的"lb"为拉丁语"libra"的缩写，等于"pound"。

7. Besides, rope and metal handle should be fixed to the cases to facilitate consignment. 而且，箱子的外层还应扣上绳子，并配上金属把手，以便于装运。
   本句中的"consignment"是"货物运输"的意思。

Sentence Menu

1. Customer's instruction to supplier

(1) As is necessary to make transshipment at Singapore for the goods to be shipped to our port, your packing must be seaworthy and strong enough to stand rough handling during transit.

(2) When packing, please take into account that the boxes are likely to receive rough handling at this end and must be able to withstand transport over every bad road.

(3) The packets must be made up in piles of suitable size before being given their air-tight tinfoil cover, and then packed in cases. The cases must be cleated and battened so as to eliminate the risk of damage caused by pressure.

(4) We usually pack each piece of men's shirt in a polybag, half dozen to a box and ten dozen to a wooden case.

(5) Packing in sturdy wooden cases is essential. Cases must be nailed, battened and secured by overall metal strapping.

(6) Our cotton prints should be packed in cases lined with draft paper and water-proof paper,

each consisting of 30 pieces in one design with 5 color-ways equally assorted.

(7) In view of the fragile nature of the goods, they should be wrapped in soft material and firmly packed in cardboard boxes so as to reduce damage in transit to a minimum.

(8) The overall measurements of each case must not exceed 1.5 m ×1 m ×1 m

- Something is supplied/packed in $\begin{cases} \text{cartons of 24} \\ \text{crate/boxes with a gross weight of ... kg.} \\ \text{strong cardboard cartons, each containing ...} \\ \text{tins which in turn contains ... each ...} \end{cases}$

- Something is wrapped/made up in water proof/waterproofed/packing material/bales measuring size 6′×3″×3″.

2. Supplier's information to customer

(1) Our usual packing for dyed poplin is in bales lined with water proof paper, each containing 500 yards in single color.

(2) We packed our shirts in plastic-lined, waterproof cartons, reinforced with metal traps.

(3) All export bicycles are wrapped in strong waterproof material at the port and packed in pairs in lightweight crates.

(4) A special crate with reinforced bottom will be needed for the transport of such a large machine, and both padding and bolting down will be essential.

(5) We will pack the material in bales of approx. 1 meter in length and 3 meters in girth. The protective canvas will be provided with ears to facilitate lifting.

(6) We regret to inform you that the goods delivered by our factory are packed single size of a box instead of assorted size as required.

(7) You will note that our packing has been greatly improved with the result that all our recent shipments have turned out to the satisfaction of our clients.

(8) You may rest assured that the packing is strong enough to withstand rough handling.

3. Instructions on shipping marks and others

(1) We give you on the attached sheet full details regarding packing and marking. These must be strictly observed.

(2) In case your shipping marks are required, your order should clearly indicate such marks and reach us one month before the shipment time.

(3) All boxes are to be marked as usual, but please number them consecutively from No. 11.

(4) The goods are to be marked with our initials in a diamond, and warning marks are to be clearly marked.

(5) The order mentioned above is completed. We are urgently awaiting your instructions regarding labeling to each package for shipment on board S.S. "Red Star".

(6) We regret being unable to accept your request for indicating the full name and address of the consignee on each package, as shipping marks comprising the initials of buyer's name will

suffice for your purpose.

(7) For dangerous and poisonous cargo, the nature and the generally adopted symbol shall be marked conspicuously on each package.

(8) Please stencil our shipping marks in letters 10 cm high, and give gross and net weight on each box.

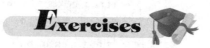

Exercises

I Put the following terms or phrases from English into Chinese or vice versa.

1. shipping mark
2. packing list
3. seaworthy packing
4. directive marks
5. consignment
6. outer packing
7. 运费
8. 中性包装
9. 发货人
10. 尺寸
11. 防水的
12. 密封的

II Fill in the blanks of the following letters with the words given below, and change the form when necessary.

> grade, transit, inform, quite, notify, place, promise, per

Dear Sirs,

Thank you for your Quotation No. 239 about Round Steel Bars.

We regret to _____ you that among the five lots of Round Steel Bars arrived here _____ S. S. "Mary" on May 11, 2015 were six bundles of different _____, which were in scattered and mixed condition because their packing was not _____ strong and their iron hoops were broken in _____. Since it was very difficult to assort them, inconvenience and losses occurred. Although we had in time _____ you of such unfortunate things occurred before, the present case has showed that our comments were ignored, for no improvement in packing has been made.

Therefore, we must have your _____ to take effective measures to improve your packing before we could _____ this new order with you.

We await your early reply.

Yours faithfully,

III Translate the following sentences into English.

1. 玻璃制品是易碎的货物，需要采取特别防止颠簸的包装措施。
2. 我方男衬衫的包装为每件套一塑料袋，5 打装一纸箱，内衬防潮纸，外打铁箍两道。
3. 我方第 125 号清洁剂用盒装，不用袋装。每盒内散装 5 公斤，然后再装入纸板箱内。这样做更适于洗衣店、医院及餐厅使用。
4. 遵照贵方要求，我们按你方来样在装袋一侧印一种颜色，但来样至少须在装运前 30 天抵达我方。
5. 所有的粉末都要用塑料袋包装，并装在罐子里，罐子盖要用胶带封紧。
6. 阀门及所有精密部件应以软材料裹住，稳固地装于硬纸盒中，纸盒放入木箱时应妥善放置，使其在箱内不可移动。

IV Writing practice.

Situational Writing 1

Write a letter to your customer informing him that you have improved your packing according to his instructions and that from today on all shirts and footwear are to be packed in cartons instead of wooden cases.

Situational Writing 2

Write a letter by making use of the following ideas.

- 本函附寄已回签了的销售合同 No. CJ -120。
- 提请对方注意以下事项：
  目的港："上海"字样须刷在每只箱子上，由于该批货物为精密仪器，还应该在箱子上刷上"DO NOT DROP"字样。
- 希望尽早得到答复。

Unit 11

Shipping

装　运

11.1　Introduction

In international trade, the exporter has various means of shipment, for instance, by ship, by truck, by train, or by airline, to ship consignment. The choice will be made according to the nature of product, the distance to be shipped, available means of transportation, time limit as well as freight cost.

One popular method of shipment is to use containers chartered from carriers. These containers vary in size, material, and construction and accommodate most cargoes, but they are best suited for standard package sizes and shapes. Also refrigerated and liquid bulk containers are usually readily available.

In case of an export business covering a large amount of goods it is necessary to make shipment in several lots by several carriers sailing on different dates. When there are no or few ships sailing direct to the port of destination at the time or the amount of cargo for a certain port of destination is so small that no ships would like to call at the port, transshipment is necessary. Of course, partial shipment and transshipment should be allowed by the buyer in advance.

Usually there are three parties involved in most transportation of goods, the consignor, the carrier and the consignee.[1] Shipment covers rather a wide range of work, such as:

(1) Buyers sending shipment instructions;
(2) Sellers sending shipping advice;
(3) Booking shipping space;
(4) Chartering ships;
(5) Appointing shipping agent;
(6) Arranging shipment;
(7) Nomination of vessels, etc.

After the shipment is made, the seller should promptly advise the buyer of its effectiveness, no matter whether the transaction is concluded on FOB, CFR, or CIF basis. For FOB and CFR transactions, the buyer will have to effect insurance to shipment upon receipt of shipping advice from the seller. It has been a customary practice that in the case of FOB transactions, the seller, before shipping, should ask the buyer to name the vessel on which the goods are to be shipped unless otherwise specified in the contract of L/C.

Letters regarding shipment are usually written for the following purposes: to urge an early shipment, to amend shipping terms, to give shipping advice, to dispatch shipping documents and so on. Taking advantage of this occasion to advise the buyer of the shipment, the seller may also review the course of the transaction and express the desire for further development of business.

11.2 Letter samples

 Letter 11-1 (Urging shipment)

Dear Sirs,

We wish to call your attention that we have extended the L/C No. 6789 for some time, but up to now we have got no definite information from you about delivery time. It may have some reasons for the delay.

It's impossible for us to extend the L/C No. 6789 again, which expires on July 5th and our customers are in urgent need of these goods.

As the long delay in delivery has caused us considerable inconvenience and loss, we ask you to deliver the goods in time, otherwise we shall cancel the orders in accordance with the stipulations of the contract.

Please make your best efforts to get the goods dispatched with the least possible delay for our long-established relationship.

Yours faithfully,

 Letter 11-2 (Urging shipment)

Dear Mr. Smith,

Our Order No. TB-286

We are now very anxious to know about the shipment of our above order for 3,000 "FeiYue" brand DVD players, which should be delivered before March 26 as contracted.

Now the shipment is approaching rapidly, but so far we have not received any information from you concerning this lot.² When we placed the order we explicitly pointed out that punctual shipment was of special importance because our customers were in urgent need of the goods and we had given them a definite assurance of early delivery.

We hope you will make every effort to effect shipment within the stipulated time as any delay would cause us inconvenience.

Sincerely yours,

 Letter 11-3（A request to advance date of shipment）

Dear Sirs,

We refer to our order No. 358 for six tons of processed polyethylene due to be shipped at the end of next month.³ When this order was placed, our stocks were considered to be sufficiently high to last until December.

However, there has been such a demand for this type of polyethylene recently that we must now ask you to arrange for immediate shipment.

As soon as we receive the above consignment we shall be in a position to judge our requirements with greater accuracy and order accordingly.

Yours faithfully,

 Letter 11-4（Proposing partial shipment）

Dear Mr. Peter,

We are pleased to receive your letter dated October 8th.

As to the issuance of L/C, we assure you that you will receive the irrevocable L/C opened by China Bank, Jiangsu Branch by the end of this month.

Regarding the delivery, as we urgently need the products to recommend to our clients, may we propose to advance the initial shipment for 50% of the total quantity from May/

June to March/April and the remaining 50% to be shipped during May/June? We can accept the transshipment terms if it is necessary and bear the extra expenses incurred.[4]

We thank you for your cooperation in advance and are looking forward to your favorable reply.

Yours sincerely,

Cheng Gang
Manager

 Letter 11-5（**Shipping instruction**）

Dear Mr. Johnson,

We thank you for your offer for 3 machine tools, and we are glad to inform you that a letter of credit in your favor has been opened last week.[5] We have booked shipping space on S.S. "Good Luck" which is due to sail from London to Dalian, Liaoning Province at the end of next month. Please get the goods ready for shipment at an early date and try your utmost to ship them by that vessel without delay.

We would like to let you know that the machines must be packed in special crates with reinforced bottom. Meanwhile, please see to it that the shipping marks indicated in our order and the gross and net weight are to be stenciled on each crate.[6]

We believe that the above instructions are clear to you and the shipment will give our users good satisfaction.

Yours sincerely,

 Letter 11-6（**Shipping advice**）

Dear Sirs,

We are pleased to have received your L/C No. 9785, covering 2,000 dozen electric drills under our Sales Confirmation No. FC9891 and inform you that shipment was loaded on M.V. "Shunfeng" on August 6 for transshipment at Singapore.

Enclosed is a set of the duplicate shipping documents, which consists of:

1. A non-negotiable copy of Bill of Lading;
2. A signed Invoice No. 889;
3. Packing list;
4. Certificate of Origin No. 1001;
5. Insurance Policy.

I would like to take this opportunity to assure you of our close cooperation.

Yours faithfully,

 Letter 11-7 (Shipping advice)

Dear Sirs,

We are writing to inform you that mowing machines have been loaded on board M.V. "Dongfeng"[7], which is scheduled to leave for Montreal on May 24, and is due by the end of this month.

We enclose our invoice and shall present shipping documents and our draft for acceptance once through the Royal Bank, Shanghai Office, as agreed.

All items were individually examined before being packed and we trust they will reach you safely. We should be pleased if you would unpack and examine them as soon as possible after delivery, and in the event of any breakage, notify us at once.

Yours faithfully,

 Letter 11-8 (Shipping advice)

Dear Mr. Goodman,

Order No. 975

We are pleased to advise you that the above order has been dispatched.

The electric drills are in fifty separate crates marked UMT IND MANILA and numbered 1 to 60.

The consignment is the M. V. "Mermaid", which left Shanghai on June 21 and is due in Manila on July 12.

We have presented to the Overseas Chinese Banking Corporation our draft for the amount of your L/C together with a full set of shipping documents consisting of Clean, Shipped on board Bills of Lading in triplicate[8], Certificate of Insurance, Certificate of Origin and our invoice in triplicate.

We hope that the drills will prove suitable for your customers' needs and look forward to receiving your next order.

Sincerely yours,

 Letter 11-9（A reply on transshipment）

Dear Sirs,

Thank you for your letter of May 21, and we are pleased to provide you the following information for your reference.

1. There are about 2 to 3 sailings weekly from Shanghai to Hong Kong.
2. Arrangements have been made with the ABCA Line, which has one sailing approximately on the 11th every month from Hong Kong to West African ports, such as Lagos, Accra, etc. Shipping space is to be booked through their Shanghai Agents, who communicate with the line by fax. After receipt of the Line's reply accepting the booking, their Shanghai Agents will issue a through bill of lading. Therefore, with the exception of unusual condition, which may happen accidentally, the goods will be transshipped from Hong Kong without delay.
3. In general the freight for transshipment from Hong Kong is higher than that from the UK or continental port, but ABCA Line agrees to the same freight, the detailed rates of which are shown on the 2 appendices to this letter.

If you want to have the goods transshipped at Hong Kong, your L/C must reach us well before the shipment month so as to enable us to book space with the Line's agents.

We assure you of our best attention at all times.

Yours faithfully,

Words and Vocabulary

charter	v.	租赁，租用
refrigerate	v.	制冷，冷冻
lot	n.	一批货
transshipment	n.	转运
book	v.	预定
nomination	n.	指定，提名
explicitly	ad.	明确地，清楚地
assurance	n.	保障，保证
advance	v.	将……提前
polyethylene	n.	聚乙烯
incur	v.	招致（损失、费用等）
reinforce	v.	加固，加强
non-negotiable	a.	不可转让的
acceptance	n.	承兑
unpack	v.	打开
freight	n.	运输费用
appendix	n.	附录
shipping terms		运输条件
shipping advice		装运通知
shipping documents		运输单据
certificate of origin		原产地证书
insurance policy		保险单
mowing machine		（草坪）割草机
Clean, Shipped on board Bills of Lading		清洁已装船提单
certificate of insurance		保险证明
shipping space		货舱
through bill of lading		联运提单

Notes

1. Usually there are three parties involved in most transportation of goods, the consignor, the carrier

and the consignee. 通常情况下，大多货物运输过程涉及三方当事人：发货人、承运人和收货人。

其中的"consignor"意思是"托运人"，"consignee"意思是"收货人"。

2. Now the shipment is approaching rapidly, but so far we have not received any information from you concerning this lot. 现在装运日快要来临了，但是我们仍未收到你方有关该批货物的任何信息。

3. We refer to our order No. 358 for six tons of processed polyethylene due to be shipped at the end of next month. 本函关于第358号订单，该订单订有6吨加工了的聚乙烯，计划于本月底装运。

本句中的"we refer to..."是外贸函电常见的开头形式，它开门见山，直奔主题，常用于关系良好的贸易双方所写的信件当中。

4. We can accept the transshipment terms if it is necessary and bear the extra expenses incurred. 如果有必要，我们愿意接受转运的条件并承担所产生的费用。

5. ... and we are glad to inform you that a letter of credit in your favor has been opened last week. 我们很高兴地通知贵方，上周已开出了以贵方为受益人的信用证。

本句中的"in your favor"是"以贵方为受益人"的意思。

6. Meanwhile, please see to it that the shipping marks indicated in our order and the gross and net weight are to be stenciled on each crate. 同时，请确认在每个板条箱子上刷上我们订单中所规定的运输标志，以及货物的毛重和净重。

7. We are writing to inform you that mowing machines have been loaded on board M.V. "Dongfeng"... 现去函告知贵方，割草机已装上"东风"号货轮……

本句中的"M.V."是"motor vessel"的缩写，即"货轮"的意思。

8. ... together with a full set of shipping documents consisting of clean, shipped on board Bills of Lading in triplicate... ……还有一整套货运单据，其中包括清洁、已装船提单，一式三份……

"in triplicate"意思为"一式三份"。其他表示"一式×份"的单词有：

duplicate（一式两份）   quadruplicate（一式四份）
quintuplicate（一式五份）   sextuplicate（一式六份）
septuplicate（一式七份）   octuplicate（一式八份）
nonuplicate（一式九份）   decuplicate（一式十份）

Sentence Menu

1. Urging shipment

(1) We regret up to the time of the writing we have not heard anything from you about the order in question.

(2) We are now referring to the Contract No. AG 6678 signed between us on 23rd April, 2015 for 1,000 cases Tin plates, which is stipulated for shipment in May 5th, 2015. However, up to now we have not received from you any information about this consignment.

(3) We wish to call your attention to the fact that up to the present moment no news comes from you about the shipment under the captioned contract.

(4) We are in urgent need of these goods and would have to request you to execute the order within the time stipulated.

(5) As the contract time of delivery is rapidly falling due, it is imperative that we hear from you without any further delay.

2. Shipping instructions

(1) We shall be very much appreciative if you effect shipment as soon as possible, thus enabling them to fill the brisk demand at the start of the season.

(2) Please try your utmost to ship our goods by S.S. "Freedom" which is due to arrive at Hamburg on September 12, and confirm by return that the goods will be ready in time.

(3) We should be much obliged if you could effect shipment of these milk power in two equal lots by direct steamer as soon as you receive our L/C.

(4) Please ensure that all the cases are marked clearly with our initials in a triangle, under which comes the destination with the contract number below.

(5) As these goods are apt to break if not handled with care in transportation, we suggest that the parcel should be sent by container vessel, to avoid possible damage in loading and discharge.

(6) The first partial goods will be shipped on the first available steamer in the middle of July. The transshipment may be allowed at Hong Kong. The port of destination is Los Angeles.

(7) It has to be stressed that shipment must be made within the prescribed time limit, as a further extension will not be considered.

(8) It is stipulated that shipment should be made before — and, if possible, we should appreciate your arranging to ship the goods at an earlier date.

(9) As the cargo is to be transshipped at Hong Kong, we shall require through Bs/L.

(10) As direct steamers to your port are few and far between, we have to ship via Hong Kong.

3. Shipping advice

(1) We are pleased to inform you that the consignment under your order No. 1129 has now been shipped per S.S. "Luck" which is to leave here on Aug. 1 and due to arrive at your port on Aug. 10, 2015.

(2) We are pleased to advise that your order for shipment per S.S. "Dove" on Aug. 23 was collected yesterday by your forwarding agent.

(3) We thank you for your letter of January 10th and now are pleased to inform you that we have

completed the above shipment in accordance with stipulation set forth in the L/C and the goods you ordered will be dispatched to you per S. S. "China Prince" tomorrow morning.

(4) In compliance with the terms of the contract, we forwarded you by airmail a full set of duplicate shipping documents immediately after the goods were shipped. The original documents are being sent to you by the Bank of China.

(5) We have shipped the above goods on board S.S. ... which will sail to your port tomorrow. Enclosed is one set of the shipping documents covering this consignment.

I Put the following terms or phrases from English into Chinese or vice versa.

1. sailing date
2. port of destination
3. order B/L
4. port of discharge
5. dock receipt
6. shipping advice
7. 运输代理
8. 舱位
9. 清洁提单
10. 船期表
11. 运输标志
12. 仓储费

II Fill in the blanks of the following letters with the words given below, and change the form when necessary.

capable, basis, part, transit, book, designate, liquefy, hitherto

Dear Sirs,

We have received your fax of March 3rd, 2015 from which we understand that you have our order for three Model 686 precision grinding machines.

Our confirmation of Order will be sent to you in a few days. The transaction of Order will be sent to you in a few days.

Since the transaction is made on FOB _____, you are to ship the goods from London on a steamer we _____. As soon as the shipping space is _____, we shall inform you of the name of the steamer, on which the goods are to go forward. For further instructions, please contact our forwarding agents, Messers. Brown Company, London, who have _____ been in charge of shipments from you.

As some parts of the machines may be damaged easily by shock, the machines must be packed in seaworthy cases _____ of withstanding rough handling. The bright metal _____ should be protected from dampness in _____ by a coating of slashing compound that will keep out dampness, but will not _____ and run off under changing weather conditions.

We believe that above instructions are very clear to you and hope that the users will be entirely satisfied with the shipment.

Yours faithfully,

III Translate the following letter into English.

敬启者：

  你方4月30日询盘已收悉，谢谢。我公司的集装箱有两种尺寸，分别为20英尺和40英尺长。集装箱两面开门，可同时进行装卸。由于装运的货物易于被湿气和水损坏，故这种集装箱具有不漏水、不透气之优点。如有必要，集装箱还可在工厂装货后锁闭，这样可避免偷窃事件发生。

  该箱有气温调控，可装需要特别照顾的任何货物。人们在装运时可充分利用其优点。

  如在同一集装箱内装有发往同一港口的几批货，可节省运费，同时还可以节省保险费用，因为集装箱运输保险费率较低。

  现随函附寄我公司费率表一份，请指示。

真诚的

IV Writing practice.

Situational Writing 1

Write an English letter with the following information given below.

Passage 1

Order No. 832, S/C No. 669703
stipulated two equal lots, Sept. and Oct., 2015-11-18
your letter of May 3rd requesting 80% June, balance July, 2015

Passage 2

Although quantity in stock too late for June shipment
especially few direct sailings
no relevant L/C yet

Passage 3

Suggesting 80% July, balance Aug., 2015

L/C June 20 latest

Prompt reply

Situational Writing 2

Read the following letter and write a reply to it.

Dear Sir or Madam:

We refer to Contract No. 6789 signed between us on Nov. 10th, 2015 for 4,500 cases Tin Plates, which is stipulated for shipment in February, 2015. However, up to the time of writing we have not received from you any information about the order in question. As you know, the contracted time of delivery is rapidly falling due and we should have received your shipping advice by the end of last month.

No doubt there must have been some reason for the delay in shipping and to cover this contingency we advised you that we were extending the Letter of Credit to the end of March. We feel sure we shall soon be hearing from you about this business.

We are awaiting your reply.

Yours truly,

Unit 12

Insurance

保 险

12.1 Introduction

Insurance is very closely related to foreign trade. In international trade, the transportation of goods from the seller to the buyer is generally over a long distance by air, by land or by sea and has to go through the procedures of loading, unloading and storing. During this process it is quite possible that the goods will encounter various kinds of perils and sometimes suffer losses. In order to protect the goods against possible losses in case of such perils, the buyer or the seller before the transportation of the goods usually applies to an insurance company for insurance covering the goods in transit.

The purpose of insurance is to provide compensation for those who suffer from loss or damage; in other words, it is a contract of indemnity, a contract to restore to someone, either the full amount of the loss that may be incurred, or a specified percentage of the amount of the loss. [1]

A contract of insurance, which is generally made in the form of an insurance policy, is one between a party who agrees to accept the risk (the insurer) and a party seeking protection from the risk (the insured). In return for payment of a premium, the insurer agrees to pay the insured a stated sum (or a proportion of it) should the event insured against occur. The premium, being the name given to the sum of money paid by the insured, is quoted at percentage of the sum insured.

There are mainly two types of insurance coverage, basic coverage and additional coverage. Basic coverage mainly includes FPA, WPA and All Risks. Additional coverage includes general additional coverage and special additional coverage. General additional coverage includes coverage of such risks as Theft, Pilferage & Non-Delivery Risks (TPND), Fresh and/or Rain Water Damage Risks, Shortage Risk, Inter-mixture & Contamination Risks, Leakage Risk, Clash & Breakage Risks, Taint of Odor Risk, Sweating & Heating Risks, Hook Damage Risk, Rust Risk, Breakage of Packing Risk. Special additional coverage covers the risks of War Risk, Strikes Risk, Failure to Delivery Risk, Import Duty Risk, On Deck Risk, Rejection Risk, etc., among which War Risk and Strike Risk are more common.

An insurance claim, if any, should be submitted to the insurance company or its agent as promptly as possible. In order to substantiate an ordinary average claim on cargo, the following documents must be presented: insurance policy or certificate, B/L, original invoice, survey report, master's protest and statement of claim.[2]

When you write a letter of covering insurance, see to it that you should write down clearly the following information: subject matter, duration of coverage, insurance amount and premium, scope of cover, etc.

12.2 Letter Samples

 Letter 12-1 (Inquiring about insurance rate)

Dear Sirs,

We will be sending a consignment of 1,000 refrigerators to Fortune Trading Company, Ltd., Pusan, the Republic of Korea. The consignment is to be loaded on to the S.S. "Prince" which sails from Xiamen on December 18 and is due in Pusan on December 23.

Details with regard to packing and values are attached, and we would be grateful if you could quote a rate covering all risks from port to port.[3]

As the matter is urgent, we would appreciate a prompt reply. Thank you.

Yours truly,

Zhang Bing
Export Manager

Attachment:

 Letter 12-2 (The reply to the inquiry about insurance rate)

Dear Mr. Zhang,

Thank you for your fax of 8 December, in which you inquired about cover for a shipment of refrigerators from Xiamen to Pushan.

I have noted from the details attached to your letter that the net amount of the invoice is US $9,000 and payment is by letter of credit. I would therefore suggest a valued policy against all risks for which we can quote 0.0058.

We will issue a cover note as soon as you complete and return the enclosed declaration form.

Yours sincerely,

 Letter 12-3（Importer asks exporter to cover insurance）

Dear Sir or Madam:

Re: Our order No. 245. Your S/C No. 867

We wish to refer you to our Order No. 245 for 1,500 cases of electric drills, from which you will see that this order was placed on CFR basis.

As we now desire to have the consignment insured at your end, we shall appreciate it if you will arrange to insure the same on behalf of us against All Risks at invoice value plus 10%, i.e. US$8,700.

We shall of course refund the premium to you upon receipt of your debit note or, if you like, you may draw on us at sight for the amount required.

We sincerely hope that our request will meet with your approval.

Yours faithfully,

 Letter 12-4（Exporter's reply about covered insurance）

Dear Sirs,

Re: Your order No. 245. Your S/C No. 867

Thank you for your letter requesting us to effect insurance on the captioned shipment for your account. We would like to inform you that we have covered the above shipment against All Risks for US$8,700 with the People's Insurance Company of China, which is a state-run enterprise enjoying high prestige in settling claims promptly and equitably. The policy is being processed and we will forward it to you by the end of the week together with our debit note for the premium.[4]

We are now making arrangements to ship your ordered consignment from Shanghai to New York, by S.S. "Dasun", sailing on or about the 15th of July.

Yours faithfully,

 Letter 12-5 (Applying for insurance)

Dear Sir or Madam:

Thank you for making your rates available to us immediately. We have obtained quotations from various insurance companies and found your quotation most competitive. After consideration, we think that the premium rate you quoted to us does not meet our expectations. Therefore, we are able to sign a general policy with your company this time.

Please insure us against All Risks at the rate of 0.005% for the sum of US$15,000 value of 1,200 sets of Changhong Color TV shipped at Qiangdao, on board S.S. "Princess", sailing for New York on July 15. Please send us the policy, together with a note for the charges.

We would be thankful if you could handle this business quickly.

Yours faithfully,

 Letter 12-6 (Asking for additional insurance)

Dear Sirs,

We have inadvertently written in our Order Confirmation No. OR231 "WPA & War Risk Insurance to be effected by sellers", whereas we should have asked for broader coverage.

Please hereafter take out cover on all our purchases of leathers against TPND, Contamination, Fresh and/or Rain Water Damage in addition to WPA.[5]

We enclose an Amendment to Order Confirmation, which is to supersede the one previously sent.

Yours faithfully,

 Letter 12-7 (Asking for the information about special rate of insurance)

Dear Sirs,

We write this letter to you in the hope of getting some information about special rate of insurance. Regularly we arrange consignment of chinaware to London by both passenger and cargo liners of the International Shipping line. Would you please tell us whether you can cover All Risks for the consignments and, if so, on what terms? Particularly, we wish to know whether you can issue a special rate for the promise of regular monthly shipments.

We are awaiting your early reply.

Yours faithfully,

 Letter 12-8 (Requiring the change of insurance clause)

Dear Sir or Madam:

We thank you for your L/C No. 168 covering glazed wall tiles. Please note that we do not cover breakage. Therefore, we hope you will delete the word "breakage" from the insurance clause in the credit. Furthermore, we have to inform you that for such articles as window glass, porcelains, etc., even if additional Risk of Breakage has been insured, the insurance is subject to a franchise of 5%. In other words, if the breakage is surveyed to be less than 5%, no claims for damage will be entertained.[6]

We believe we have now made our position clear. Please fax the amendment immediately.

Yours faithfully,

Unit 12 Insurance

 Letter 12-9（A reply to the claim）

Dear Mr. Cooke,

Policy No. EIL3258

I have now received our assessor's report with reference to your claim CR8653 in which you asked for compensation for damage to two marble polishers, which were shipped ex-Qingdao on the S. S. "Taishan" on May 5th, for delivery to your customer, Hitek Industries, Bangkok.

The report states that the B/L, No. 5326, was claused by the captain of the vessel, with a comment on cracks in the cashing of the machinery.[7]

Our assessor believes that these cracks were responsible for the casing weakening during the voyage and splitting, which eventually caused damage to the polishers themselves.

I am sorry that we cannot help you further, but the company cannot accept liability for goods[8] unless they are shipped clean. See clause 13C of the Policy.

Yours sincerely,

Words and Vocabulary

procedure	n.	程序，手续
encounter	v.	遭遇，遇见
peril	n.	风险，危险
indemnity	n.	赔偿
substantiate	v.	证实，证明（控诉、主张等）有根据
protest	n.	拒付证书，船长证明书
duration	n.	期限，期间
refund	v.	偿还债务
prestige	n.	名誉，名声
equitably	ad.	公平地
inadvertently	ad.	不经意地，疏忽地
supersede	v.	替代，代替

153

chinaware	n.	陶器
breakage	n.	破碎，破损
porcelain	n.	瓷器
assessor	n.	货损评估师
liability	n.	责任

FPA	平安险
WPA	水渍险
All Risks	一切险
TPND (Theft, Pilferage & Non-Delivery Risks)	偷窃提货不着险
Fresh and/or Rain Water Damage Risks	淡水雨淋险
Shortage Risk	（缺）短量险
Inter-mixture & Contamination Risks	混杂污损险
Leakage Risk	渗漏险
Clash & Breakage Risks	破损破碎险
Taint of Odor Risks	串味险
Sweating & Heating Risks	受潮受热险
Hook Damage Risks	钩损险
Rust Risk	锈损险
Breakage of Packing Risk	包装破碎险
special additional coverage	特殊附加险
War Risk	战争险
Strike Risk	罢工险
Failure to Delivery Risk	交货不到险
Import Duty Risk	进口关税险
On Deck Risk	舱面险
Rejection Risk	拒收险
master's protest	船长声明书
declaration form	启运通知单
electric drill	电动钻头
invoice value	发票金额
debit note	借项清单
general policy	大保单
amendment to order confirmation	订单确认修改书
cargo liner	货运班轮
glazed wall tile	琉璃瓦
marble polisher	大理石刨光机

Unit 12 Insurance

1. ... in other words, it is a contract of indemnity, a contract to restore to someone, either the full amount of the loss that may be incurred, or a specified percentage of the amount of the loss. ……换句话说,保险是赔偿的合同,它能使受损方挽回全部损失或合同中所规定的一定比例的损失。

    本句中的"restore to someone"是"恢复某人的损失到……状态"的意思。

2. In order to substantiate an ordinary average claim on cargo, the following documents must be presented: insurance policy or certificate, B/L, original invoice, survey report, master's protest and statement of claim. 为了使货物损失的索赔具有依据,必须提供下列单据:保险单或保险证明、提单、原始货物发票、货损评估报告、船长声明书及索赔要求。

3. Details with regard to packing and values are attached, and we would be grateful if you could quote a rate covering all risks from port to port. 本函附寄了有关包装和货物价值的一些材料。如果卖方能报出从港口到港口一切险的保险费率,本公司将不胜感激。

    本句中的"with regard to"是"有关,关于"的意思。

4. The policy is being processed and we will forward it to you by the end of the week together with our debit note for the premium. 本保险单正在缮制,在本周末我们将寄送给你方该保险单,以及保险费的借项清单。

5. Please hereafter take out cover on all our purchases of leathers against TPND, Contamination, Fresh and/or Rain Water Damage in addition to WPA. 在此我们将根据偷窃提货不着险、玷污险、淡水雨淋险及水渍险,对我们所购买的皮革制品投保。

    本句中的"purchases"意思是"所购买的货物"。

6. ... even if additional Risk of Breakage has been insured, the insurance is subject to a franchise of 5%. In other words, if the breakage is surveyed to be less than 5%, no claims for damage will be entertained. ……即使已投了破碎险,但是保险的免赔率为5%。换言之,如果货物的破损率低于5%,是不予理赔的。

7. The report states that the B/L, No. 5326, was claused by the captain of the vessel, with a comment on cracks in the cashing of the machinery. 从报告上看到,货船的船长曾在5326号提单上加注批语,称机器的包装箱上有裂缝。

    本句中的"claused B/L"即为"unclean B/L",意为"非清洁提单"。

8. ... but the company cannot accept liability for goods ... ……但是我们公司不能接受对货物的赔偿责任……

Sentence Menu

1. Asking for insurance

(1) I am looking for insurance from your company, and I want to know what types of cover you usually underwrite.

(2) The goods are ready for shipment and we wish to cover insurance for the consignment.

(3) For the shipment in question, our clients request you to cover insurance against WPA.

(4) We are willing to take out FPA and WPA covers for the shipment. Would you please give us the policy rates for FPA coverage and for WPA coverage?

(5) Will you please arrange to take out all-risks insurance for us on the following consignment of electronic pumps from our warehouse at the above address to Boston.

(6) Please effect insurance for our account of GBP 6,000 on our goods against WPA and War Risk from Shanghai to Liverpool, and at the lowest premium possible, not exceeding 10%.

(7) We would like to know whether you can undertake insurance on wine against All Risks, including breakage and pilferage risks.

(8) We would be obliged if you can hold us covered for the cargo listed on the attached sheet.

(9) We are making regular shipments from ... to ... and should be glad to hear whether you would be prepared to issue an open policy.

(10) According to our usual practice we prefer our export shipment to be insured by the People's Insurance Company of China.

(11) Will you please quote us a rate for the insurance against All Risks of a shipment of ... to ... by S.S. ... The invoice value is ...

(12) If you wish to secure protection against TPND, it can be easily done upon the payment of an additional premium.

2. Asking for extra insurance

(1) For a shipment of this nature, WPA is too narrow. You are requested to extend coverage to include TPND.

(2) I now wish to increase the amount of cover from its current figure of CAN$ 25,000 to $ 30,000 with immediate effect.

(3) Owing to the fact that these bags have occasionally been dropped into the water during loading and unloading, the insurers have raised the premium to ...%. We, therefore, think that it would be to your advantage to have WPA coverage instead of the FPA.

(4) If you desire to cover ... we can provide such coverage at a slightly higher premium.

(5) We should have asked for broader coverage. Please hereafter take out cover on all our

purchases of leathers against TPND, Contamination, Fresh and/or Rain Water Damage in addition to WPA.

3. Replies to the insurance request

(1) For transactions concluded on FOB and CFR basis, insurance is to be covered by buyers for CIF sales, insurance is to be covered by sellers for 110% of the invoice value against the risks specified in the contract.

(2) Should you so desire, we shall insure these goods at your cost.

(3) If the business is concluded on CIF basis, we generally insure WPA; other special risks such as TPND, leakage, breakage, freshwater, oil grease, etc. can be covered upon request.

(4) We have pleasure in informing you that we have insured your Order No. SH1606 for the invoice cost plus 20% up to the port of destination.

(5) In the absence of your definite instructions regarding the insurance, we have covered the goods you ordered against WPA for 110% of the invoice value according to our usual practice.

(6) Breakage is a special risk, for which an extra premium will have to be charged. The additional premium is for the buyer's account.

(7) Insurance on the goods shall be covered by us for 110% of the CIF value, and any extra premium for additional coverage, if required, shall be borne by the buyers.

(8) Regarding insurance, the coverage is for 110% of invoice value up to the port of destination only.

(9) We regret being unable to agree to the buyer's request as stated in the L/C stipulations for insurance to be covered up to the island city because our price is based on CIF Hong Kong.

(10) Owing to the risk of war, we cannot accept the insurance at the ordinary rate. At the same time, it would be to your advantage to have particular average cover.

(11) Our terms of insurance is to be effected by the sellers for 110% of invoice value against All Risks and War Risk.

I Put the following terms or phrases from English into Chinese or vice versa.

1. insurance rate
2. FPA
3. TPND
4. open policy
5. general average
6. insurance claim
7. 保险费
8. 中国保险条款
9. 相对免赔额
10. 特殊附加险

11. 仓至仓条款　　　　　　　　12. 保险索赔

II **Fill in the blanks of the following letter with the words and expressions given, and change the form where necessary.**

> conclude, as per, comply, so, should, make, accordingly, account, in, bear

Dear Sirs,

In reply to your letter of the 3rd November inquiring about the insurance on our CIF offer for cosmetics _____ to you on 12th November, we wish to give you the following information.

For transactions _____ on CIF basis, we usually effect insurance with the People's Insurance Company of China against All Risks, _____ Ocean Marine Cargo Clause of the People's Insurance Company of China, dated the 1st January, 1981. _____ you require the insurance to be covered as per Institute Cargo Clauses, we would be glad to _____. But if there is any difference in premium between the two it will be charged to your _____.

We are also _____ a position to insure the shipment against any additional risks if you _____ desire, and the extra premium is to be _____ by you. In this case, we shall send you the premium receipt issued by the relative underwriter.

Usually, the amount insured is 110% of the total invoice value. However, if a higher percentage is required, we may do _____ but you have to bear the extra premium as well.

We hope our above information will provide you with all that you wish to know and we are now looking forward to receiving your order.

Yours faithfully,

III **Put the following sentences into the right order to make a complete letter.**

1. As discussed in our e-mail, we now desire to have the order insured at your side.
2. We sincerely hope our request will meet your approval.
3. Referring to our Purchase Contract No. BT-67 for 300 Shandong Groundnuts, you will see the transaction is concluded on CFR basis.
4. We will refund the premium to you upon receipt of your draft at sight on us or a debit note.
5. We shall very much appreciate it if you could have the goods covered for our account against FPA and Aflatoxin Risk for 110% of the invoice value, totally GBP 55,000.
6. Looking forward to your early reply

Unit 12　Insurance

IV Translate the following sentences into English.

1. 我们要为这批货投保平安险和水渍险，请告知上述两种险别的保险费率。
2. 破损险是一种特殊险，需要为此支付额外保险费，其增加的保险费由买方负担。
3. 我方将在此按我方的预约保单办理保险。
4. 保险费随着承保范围的不同而不同，如果需投保附加险，额外保险费将由买方承担。
5. 我们很遗憾地得知你方货物在途中严重受损，保险公司将按照投保险别赔偿损失。
6. 在CIF的基础上售出的货物，我们通常按发票金额加成10%投保一切险和战争险。
7. 我们将保险事宜留给你方安排，我们希望这些货物投保一切险和战争险。
8. 我们企业是一家国有企业，享有理赔迅速、公正的声誉，并在世界上主要的港口和地区都设有代理处。

V Writing practice.

Situational Writing

Write an English Letter based on the following particulars.

- 通知对方所订30箱摄像机（camcorders）将由"东风"号轮于本月底或下月初运出。
- 告诉对方将根据此批货物的性质，代对方投保一切险。
- 如对方有什么异议，请赶紧告知。

Unit 13

Complaints and Claims
投诉与索赔

13.1 Introduction

In business activities, no matter how perfect an organization may be, complaints from the customers are certain to arise. Generally speaking, complaints may be of several kinds, and may arise from the delivery of wrong goods, damaged goods, or too many or too few goods or quality may have been found unsatisfactory, and etc.

If a complaint or claim has to be made by the buyer, the matter should be investigated in detail and these details should be laid before the party charged.

We must handle complaints or claims in accordance with the principle of "on the first grounds, to our advantage and with restraint" and settle them amicably to the satisfaction of all parties concerned.[1] Usually a complaint or claim letter should follow the following principle.

(1) Begin by regretting the need to complain.
(2) Mention the date of the order, the date of delivery and the goods complained about.
(3) State your reasons for being dissatisfied and ask for an explanation.
(4) Refer to the inconvenience caused.
(5) Suggest how the matter should be put right.
(6) We must also be careful in choosing the wording in our correspondence so as to avoid any misunderstandings.

Sometimes, a reference to the previously satisfactory deliveries and services may help to win more sympathetic consideration of the present complaint or claim.

Having been given a complaint or claim letter by the buyer, the seller should deal with the matter according to the following rules without delay.

(1) The first thing that has to be decided is whether the complaint is justified.
(2) If so, then you have to admit it readily, express your regret and promise to put the matter right.
(3) If the complaint is not justified, point out politely and in an agreeable manner. It would be

a wrong policy to refuse the claim offhand.

(4) If you cannot deal with a complaint promptly, acknowledge it at once. Explain that you are looking into it and that you will send a full reply later.

(5) All complaints should be treated as serious matters and thoroughly investigated.

Letters concerning disputes should be written tactfully and reasonably. They must be confined to a statement of facts and insist on the absolute truth.

13.2 Letter Samples

 Letter 13-1 (Complaint about low quality)

Dear Sirs,

The green beans under S/C No. ED034 dispatched on May 4th, 2015 arrived at our port last week. The Commodity Inspection Bureau has carefully examined the quality of the beans, and we regret to say that they found it is far below the standard stipulated in the S/C and the covering Inspection Certificate is going to be airmailed to you as soon as it comes to hand.

We think you will look into the matter at once and take immediate measures to correct the mistakes and ensure that nothing like this will happen in the future.

The inferior quality of these beans causes us considerable difficulty and it is hard for us to dispose of it, even at a rather low price. We think we can reserve the right to lodge a claim against you for the loss we have suffered.[2]

Yours faithfully,

 Letter 13-2 (Reply to complaint about low quality)

Dear Sirs,

We are sorry to learn from your letter of May 28th, 2015 that the green beans dispatched on May 4th, 2015 were below the standard stipulated in the contract and that you are reserving the right to lodge a claim against us.

Naturally we hope that the transaction will be concluded to your satisfaction. Now that you have found the quality of the beans do not comply with that stipulated in the contract, we want to have the problem clarified without any delay. So we have sent our representative to your end to investigate the matter in detail.³ We would not give any comments before our representative inspects the goods. We will soon let you know the date of his visit and hope you will give him your best cooperation.

You may be assured that the matter will be settled in a reasonable manner to our mutual benefits.

Yours faithfully,

 Letter 13-3（Further reply by exporter）

Dear Sir or Madam:

We have got the news from our representative that through his careful study he has found deterioration of a very small part of the green beans delivered on May 4th, 2015, under the S/C No. ED034. First please accept our sincere apologies for the inconvenience caused to you.

Nevertheless, as you may be aware such deterioration can hardly be avoided during the long period of transportation and storage. We hope that you will not take this case as a breach of the contract and refrain from making any claims against us as the loss can be negligible⁴, and you know well, in fact, we have delivered more quantities than that stipulated.

Please be assured that in our future business, we will take great measures to ensure nothing like this to happen again.

Yours faithfully,

 Letter 13-4（Complaining about delay in shipment）

Dear Sirs,

We enclose herewith the figures of sales in your product during the past six months, from which you will see that our sales of the special line are quite disappointing.

Because the end-users here are in urgent need of the goods, we requested your prompt shipment of them, which you had accepted. However, five weeks went by before the goods arrived instead of three weeks, and we lost a wonderful opportunity of sales.

On inquiry we found that the goods were not shipped until four weeks after the date of dispatch. We have been put to considerable inconvenience through long delay and have to ask you to make us allowance corresponding to our loss.[5]

Yours faithfully,

  Letter 13-5 (Apologizing for the delay in shipment)

Dear Sirs,

We have received your letter complaining our delay of shipment, and we are very sorry that we have not been able to deliver your order on time. The delay was caused by the late arrival of some of the raw materials.

It is due to the events that are entirely beyond our control. We are pleased, however, that your order will be ready for shipment next week, and we hope that they will arrive in time for the season. Please accept our apologies to you for the delay and the inconvenience it has caused you.

Yours faithfully,

  Letter 13-6 (Complaining about poor packing)

Dear Sirs,

We regret to inform you that the cotton goods covered by our Order No. 8632 and shipped per S.S. "Peace" arrived in such an unsatisfactory condition that we cannot but lodge a complaint against you. It was found, upon examination, that nearly 20% of the packages had been broken, obviously attributed to improper packing. Our only recourse, in consequence, was to have them repacked before delivering to our customers, which inevitably resulted in extra expenses amounting to US$ 860.⁶ We expect compensation from you for this, and should like to take this opportunity to suggest that special care be taken in your future deliveries as prospective customers are apt to misjudge the quality of your goods by the faulty packing.

Yours faithfully,

 Letter 13-7（**Replying to complaint about alleged poor packing**）

Dear Sirs,

We thank you for your letter of May 11th, 2015 and are sorry to note your complaint about the cotton goods we sent you by S. S. "Peace". We can assure you, however, that the goods in question were in perfect order when they left here, hence the damage complained of must have occurred in transit. In these circumstances, we are apparently not liable for the damage and would advise you to claim on the shipping company who should be held responsible.

At any rate, we deeply regret to learn from you about this unfortunate incident and should it be necessary, we shall be pleased to take the matter up on your behalf with the shipping company concerned.⁷

Yours faithfully,

 Letter 13-8（**Claim for shortweight and inferior quality**）

Dear Sirs,

We are writing to you about the fertilizers shipped per S.S. "Far East" in execution of Contract No. HB-8341, and discharged at Tianjin, and we now lodge claims with you as follows:

Claim Number	Claim For	Amount
DEC-41	Short-weight	US$ 2,358
DEC-42	Quality	US$ 12,563
	Total Amount	US$ 14,957

To support our claims, we enclose herewith one copy each of Inspection Certificate No. 82012 and No. 82013 together with our statement of claims, which amounts to US$ 14,957.

We feel sure that you will give our claims your most favorable consideration and let us have your settlement soon.

Yours faithfully,

 Letter 13-9（**Reply to the above letter**）

Dear Sirs,

Ref: Contract No. HB-8341

We have received your letter of July 5th, 2015 with enclosures, claiming for shortage in weight and inferior quality on the consignment of fertilizers shipped per S.S. "Far East".

We immediately looked into the matter and found that our fertilizers were properly weighed at the time of loading and the quality was up to standard. We, on our part, really cannot account for the reason of your complaint. But since the fertilizers were examined by a public surveyor upon arrival at Tianjin, we cannot but accept your claim as tendered.

We therefore enclose our check No. 6635 for US$ 14,957 in full and final settlement of your claims DEC-41 and 42. Kindly acknowledge receipt at your convenience.

We apologize for the trouble caused to you and would like to assure you that all possible steps will be taken by us to avoid any recurrence of similar nature in our future dealings with you.

Yours truly,

 Letter 13-10（**Claim for damages**）

Dear Sirs,

The captioned goods you shipped per S.S. "Changhong" on May 14 arrived here yesterday.[8] On examination, we have found that many of the electric heaters are severely damaged, though the cases themselves show no trace of damage.

Considering this damage was due to the rough handling by the shipping company, we claim on them for recovery of loss; but an investigation made by the surveyor has revealed the fact that the damage is attributable to improper packing. For further particulars, we refer you to the surveyor's report enclosed.

We are therefore, compelled to claim on you to compensate us for the loss, US$ 20,000, which we have sustained by the damage to the goods.

We trust that you will be kind enough to accept this claim and deduct the sum claimed from the amount of your next invoice to us.

Yours faithfully,

Letter 13-11 (Reply to claim for damages)

Dear Sirs,

We have received your letter of 5th July, informing us that the electric heaters we shipped to you arrived damaged on account of improper packing on our part.⁹

On receiving your letter, we have given this matter our immediate attention. We have studied your surveyor's report very carefully.

We are convinced that the present damage was due to extraordinary circumstances under which they were transported to you. We are therefore not responsible for the damage; but as we do not think that it would be fair to have you bear the loss alone, we suggest that the loss be divided between both of us, to which we hope you will agree.

Faithfully yours,

Words and Vocabulary

amicably	ad.	友好地
inconvenience	n.	不方便

Unit 13 Complaints and Claims

sympathetic	a.	同情的，富有同情心的
justify	v.	认为……是合理的
tactfully	ad.	有策略地
inferior	a.	低一等的，劣质的，不合要求的
considerable	a.	大量的
reserve	v.	保留
deterioration	n.	恶化，降级，食物变质
breach	n.	违反（合同）
refrain	v.	克制
negligible	a.	可忽视的，不予重视的
herewith	ad.	与此一道
end-user	n.	最终用户
misjudge	v.	误读，误判
alleged	a.	声称的
shortweight	a.	短量的
fertilizer	n.	化肥
tender	v.	（正式）提出
recurrence	n.	再次发生
compelled	a.	被迫的
deduct	v.	从……扣除
extraordinary	a.	特别的，特殊的
dispose of		处理，安排
to lodge a claim against		向……起诉
comply with		与……一致
to your end		在你方
refrain from		克制住
in consequence		结果
in perfect order		完好无损
electric heater		电热器

Notes

1. We must handle complaints or claims in accordance with the principle of "on the first grounds, to our advantage and with restraint" and settle them amicably to the satisfaction of all parties concerned.　我们必须依据"实事求是，互惠互利，克制谦让"的原则友好地处理投诉事宜，使有关方都感到满意。

本句中的"to our advantage"相当于"to our benefit",意为"互惠互利"。

2. We think we can reserve the right to lodge a claim against you for the loss we have suffered.
   我们认为我们保留向你方起诉进行索赔的权利。
   本句中的"reserve the right"为"保留权利"的意思。

3. So we have sent our representative to your end to investigate the matter in detail.
   因此我们便派代表去你方详细调查此事。
   本句中的"to your end"是"去你方,去你公司所在地"意思。

4. We hope that you will not take this case as a breach of the contract and refrain from making any claims against us as the loss can be negligible... 我们希望你方不要将此事视为违约,也不要提出索赔,因为这些损失是可以忽略不计的……
   本句中的"refrain from"为"抑制,忍住"等意思。

5. We have been put to considerable inconvenience through long delay and have to ask you to make us allowance corresponding to our loss. 货物的长期延误已经给我们公司造成许多不便,我们不得不要求你方对我们的损失予以赔偿。
   本句中的"make us allowance"是"给我们补偿、赔偿"的意思,"corresponding to"是"根据,依据"的意思。

6. Our only recourse, in consequence, was to have them repacked before delivering to our customers, which inevitably resulted in extra expenses amounting to US$ 860. 因此,我们唯一的补救办法就是在将货物发往我们的顾客之前,必须对货物进行重新包装,这将会产生860美元的额外费用。

7. ... and should it be necessary, we shall be pleased to take the matter up on your behalf with the shipping company concerned. ……如果有必要的话,我们非常愿意代表贵公司与有关货运公司对此事进行交涉。
   本句中的"should it be necessary"为虚拟语气,等于"if it is necessary"的意思。

8. The captioned goods you shipped per S. S. "Changhong" on May 14 arrived here yesterday. 本标题所述货物于5月14日由"长虹"号轮装运,已于昨天到达本地。

9. We have received your letter of 5th July, informing us that the electric heaters we shipped to you arrived damaged on account of improper packing on our part. 我们已收悉贵方7月5日来信,得知我方发运的电取暖器由于包装不当,到达时已有损坏。
   本句中的"on account of"是"由于,因为"的意思。

1. Complaints about quality and replies

(1) Upon examination, we found that many of the goods were severely damaged, though the cases showed no trace of damage.

(2) Although the quality of these goods is not up to that of our usual lines, we are prepared to

accept them if you will reduce the prices, say, by . . .

(3) We are sorry to inform you that your last shipment is not of your usual standard. The goods seem to be too roughly made and are inclined to be inferior and out of shape.

(4) We regret to have to inform you that the computers, which you sold us on . . . has caused numerous complaints.

(5) Upon examination, we have found that the quality of the products is too inferior to meet the requirement at our local market.

(6) You must clearly understand that unless what you can supply is with the best quality in every case, we shall have to fill our requirements elsewhere.

(7) We were sorry to receive your complaint that the material you received was not of the quality expected.

(8) Needles to say, we are most willing to replace the faulty articles.

2. Complaints about poor packing and replies

(1) We have examined them one by one, and found that each of them was leaking more or less.

(2) In our opinion, the damage was caused by improper packing. A machine of this size and weight should be blocked in position inside the export case.

(3) The packing inside was too loose with result that there was some shifting of the contents and several cups and plates have been broken. The attached list will give you details.

(4) We have had the case and its contents examined by the insurance surveyor but, as you will see from the enclosed copy of this report, he maintains that the damage was probably due to insecure packing and not to any unduly rough handling of the case.

(5) The cases were found to be badly damaged. This was apparently attributable to faulty packing.

(6) We are sorry that we cannot accept your claim because the cases were damaged in the transit, which should be the responsibility of the shipping forwarder.

(7) We are sorry that we cannot bear the responsibility for the damages incurred to your goods, because we have the documents to prove that the goods were received by the carrier in perfection.

3. Complaints about shortages and replies

(1) In checking the contents against your enclosed invoice, it was found that several items were missing.

(2) There is a discrepancy between the packing list of case No. 56 and your invoice; 3 dozen Tea Sets are correctly entered on the invoice but there were only 2 dozen in the case.

(3) The Inspection Certificate shows that there is a shortage of 561 kilos, which in the opinion of the Bureau had occurred before shipment because the packing remained intact when the parcel was landed at our port. Would you please send us a check for US$ 15,00 to cover

this shortage and the Inspection fee of US$ 250?

(4) The alleged shortage might have occurred in the course of transit, and that is a matter over which we can excise no control.

(5) We would like to compensate you for the shortage in weight mentioned in your letter of ... percent by offering you an allowance of ... percent.

4. Complaints about delay in shipment and replies

(1) This delay has inconvenienced us considerably. We should appreciate it if you would inform us by return mail when we may expect the goods.

(2) For the past weeks we have been urging you for an immediate dispatch of these goods, and unless this order is already on the way, it will arrive too late for the season, and so be of no use to us.

(3) We trust you will now consider this matter seriously and make an effort to prevent the reoccurrence of this annoying delay.

(4) Please inform us soon whether you can deliver the goods by the end of July. If your answer is the negative, we shall have to cancel the order as we cannot possibly wait any longer.

(5) As you know, the demand for these goods is seasonal. We shall, therefore, be forced to cancel this order and buy elsewhere unless we can get immediate shipment.

(6) Due to your excessive delay in delivery, we notify you of our cancellation of contract.

(7) As the time of shipment is now considered overdue, we hope you will inform us by return of the reason for delay.

(8) The delay on your part has already put us in a very serious and awkward position toward our customers, and we must ask you kindly to do your best to help us out of it.

(9) Please take the matter up at once and see to it that the goods are delivered without delay.

(10) The goods are promised to be delivered within ... and we have been put to considerable inconvenience through the long delay.

5. Complaints about wrong goods and replies

(1) We are sorry to inform you that you have sent us the wrong goods, and this error is inconvenient and annoying to us.

(2) On going into the matter we find a mistake was indeed made in the packing through a confusion in numbers, and we have arranged for the right goods to be dispatched to you at once.

(3) Upon examining your first delivery, we find that it does not contain the assortment which we ordered.

(4) We have found that the goods shipped to us in execution of our Order No. 35/26 do not correspond with the sample, which led to our placing the order. You should explain the reason on the matter.

(5) Unfortunately, we find that the bulk of the goods delivered is not up to sample.

I Put the following terms or phrases from English into Chinese or vice versa.

1. faulty packing
2. force majeure
3. breach of the contract
4. short weight
5. inspection report
6. shoddy goods
7. 理赔
8. 仲裁条款
9. 不履行合同
10. 取消订单
11. 做工低劣
12. 诉讼

II Fill in the blanks of the following letter with the words and expressions given, and change the form where necessary.

> make, in, instant, far, forward, due, amply, with, inconvenience, late

Dear Mr. Xia,

We have received your fax of 2nd March, and very much regret the delay _____ delivering the above. We are now _____ the necessary arrangements for immediate delivery, which means you will have both excavators by 20th March at the latest.

The HERCULES JBM is the most successful excavator we have so _____ produced. It was an _____ success at its first appearance last year at the Hong Kong Building Exhibition and we were soon inundated _____ orders. Your own order was received in November and according to the waiting list we had then was not _____ for delivery until April. Nevertheless, we put the delivery date _____ so that you would have the machines in March. In February production was slightly set back by the _____ arrival of some special parts and this has been responsible for the delay in the present case.

We trust that you will not be unduly _____ by having to wait a few more days. The performance of the HERCULES JBM excavators will _____ compensate you.

Yours sincerely,

III Rearrange the following paragraphs in a logic order to make them a perfect letter.

1. We are looking forward to receiving your remittance we are due to get.
2. You are perfectly correct in saying that packing and insurance are normally less for air cargo. However, we remind you that your request to send the goods by air was made at very short notice. It was impossible for us to use the lighter airfreight packing materials. Furthermore, our insurance is on open policy, and depends on the value of the goods, not on the method of transportation.
3. We have read carefully your letter of complaint on the discrepancy of the goods with the original sample. This was apparently caused by the oversight of our production department. Please allow us to offer an apology for your inconvenience. We are sending you a new lot by air at once, and would ask you to return the faulty goods at your convenience with freight forward or you may keep them for sale at a reduced price of 34% discount.

IV Translate the following letter into English.

敬启者：

  你方7月16日关于本公司交货服务质量问题之来函已收悉，十分感谢你方提出使我们注意的有关事项。我能够理解延迟交货给你方造成的巨大损失。

  我们向运输公司做了核实，近几次交货确有延误，让你方久等，我们对此也难以接受。对于此事给你方带来的不便，本人深表歉意。我向你方保证我们正在考虑更换运输公司，以避免此类错误再次发生。

  我们素来重视客户的意见。本着这一原则，我们非常乐意对贵公司此次订货（No. 73522）做出特别安排，在三天之内发货。

  对贵公司所添加的麻烦，谨再次由衷致歉。

敬上

V Writing practice.

Situational Writing 1

Your company ordered from New Century Company 60 sets of air conditioners. They included 30 sets of Model A and 30 sets of Model B. But when the goods arrived, you found that there were 25 sets of Model A and 35 sets of Model B. **You are now requested to write to Mr. Peter, sales manager of New Century Company and complain about the wrong delivery of the goods.**

Unit 13 Complaints and Claims

Situational Writing 2

Suppose your company had just received 40 sets of machines, 4 of which had been found inferior in quality. **You are requested to write a letter of claim against the supplier, ABR Machine Company on the poor quality of the machines.**

Situational Writing 3

Your company got a letter of complaint in which your client stated that you had delivered one wrong case of goods. **Now you are requested to write a reply to inform that you are going to deliver the correct goods to substitute the wrong case and the relevant documents will be soon prepared. The costs of the shipment will be borne by your company.**

Unit 14

Agency
代　　理

14.1　Introduction

　　Many transactions in international trade are handled not only by direct negotiations between buyers and sellers but by means of agencies. A foreign agent is well familiar with the local business environment, and knows clearly what goods are needed and what prices are the best in the local market, therefore, it may be convenient and economical for a company to do business through agencies.[1]

　　An agency is an organization, especially a company, acting as the representative, agent, or subcontractor of a person or another company.[2] It indicates a legal relationship involving a person or an organization and another who acts for the person or the organization. The person or the organization that empowers another to conduct business performance is called the principal, and the empowered is termed the agency. The most prominent feature of this form of business in international trade is that the principal enters into relations with the customers abroad by the agent who is on behalf of the principal but is not his employee.[3]

　　Generally, there are two main types of agencies: the exclusive agency and the non-exclusive agency. The exclusive agency, also known as the sole agency, is a firm or a person who acts for his foreign principal with exclusive rights to sell in a specific area on a commission basis and he will not sell products that compete with the products of the principal. The non-exclusive agency, also called the general agent, is a firm or a person who acts under instructions from his principal to sell or buy on the best terms obtainable and who may sell or buy the competitors' goods.[4] Mostly, a principal has only one agency in a certain area, and cannot empower other people or organizations the same rights in that area.

　　The principal should make careful investigations about the prospective agencies, and has to make sure the firm or person to be appointed has sufficient means to develop the trade and reliable connections in the designated area. The company should also make inquires into the qualifications, experiences and other necessary information of the agent candidates, such as the reliability and financial soundness, their market connections and sales channels[5], and whether they are agents of the principal's competitors. Though the terms of agency vary with different circumstances, they should be made clear and definite, particularly for dealings involving large sales. A formal agreement on agency may include the following items: the nature and duration of the agency, the territory to be covered, the duties of the parties concerned, the method of purchase and sale, and the commission for the agency.[6]

14.2 Letter Samples

 Letter 14-1（Looking for an agent）

Dear Sirs,

There has been a steady increase in demand for our porcelain products in the last six months, so we have decided to appoint an agent to handle our export trade with your country. We understand you specialize in porcelain products and are writing to ask if you would be interested in marketing our products in your country on a commission basis.[7]

We know you have wide experiences and connections in the porcelain trade. We believe your firm is the right one we are looking for, and we have great pleasure in offering you a sole agency. Attached is our catalogue, which will show you the wide range of our products.

If you decide to accept our request and be our sole agency, please state the terms on which you would be willing to represent us.

Yours faithfully,

Clifford V. Johnson

 Letter 14-2（Asking to be sales agent）

Dear Sirs,

We are interested in your wine products and would be very happy to offer our services as your agent in Egypt.

We are one of the largest firms in the wine and spirit trade in Egypt. We have better knowledge of the market here and good and effective distributing channels.⁸ There is a growing demand here for Chinese wine since more and more Chinese visitors and businessmen have come to Egypt. We had some kind of your wine products at a banquet last week and were impressed by its unique taste and smell. If you give us an opportunity to be your agent, we think it will be a mutual-benefit deal. When we have details of your ranges with samples and prices, we shall advise you of their suitability for this market and choose the types that are likely to sell well.

As to our financial standing and reliability, you may refer to our bank or to any of our major customers. They will offer you the first-class references that prove us agents of high integrity.⁹

We are looking forward to your favorable reply.

Yours faithfully,

Arthur Goldschmidt

Letter 14-3 (Favorable reply to a letter asking to be an agent)

Dear Sirs,

We wish to thank you for your letter of December 17, in which you offer your services as our agent in Egypt, and are favorably impressed with your firm after connecting with our bank in Cairo. We understand you are a reliable and well-established firm with good credit and integrity.

We would like to inform you that we have decided to entrust you with the sole agency for our wine products in the territory of Egypt.

The agency agreement has been drawn up for a duration of one year, automatically renewable on expiration for a similar period unless a written notice is given the contrary.¹⁰ Attached is a copy of the draft. We will send you samples of our products immediately when we receive your favorable reply.

We are looking forward to your early reply.

Yours faithfully,

Bruce Du

Unit 14 Agency

 Letter 14-4（Declining an agent application）

Dear Sirs,

We thank you for your inquiry regarding sole agency for the sale of our wine products.

We appreciate your offering, but we decided not to commit ourselves at this stage when the record of transactions shows only a moderate volume of business.[11] However, this does not imply we are dissatisfied. Actually, we are quite satisfied with your cooperation and assistance over the past years in the sales of our wine products.

In our opinion, a bigger turnover must be reached to justify establishing an agency and it would be better for us to postpone the agency matter until your future sales warrant such a step. Besides, it would be necessary for you to test the marketability of our products at your end and to build a larger turnover to justify the agency arrangements.

We hope that you will understand our position and continue giving us your cooperation and assistance.

Yours faithfully,

Ross Liang

 Letter 14-5（Reply to an offer of agency）

Dear Sirs,

We have received your letter dated January 29 and thank you for the confidence you show in us by offering us a sole agency in Norway for your range of porcelain wares.

There is an increasing demand for your porcelain products in Europe. However, people here are not so acquainted with the your special craftsmanship and painting style, and it would be necessary to launch an advertising campaign to promote your products. Also you have to face the competition of producers from South Asia and Egypt in the porcelain ware market.

We are willing to give it a trial if you would like to organize the advertising campaign and bear the costs incurred in the first year. Obviously, our understanding of Chinese culture may not be correct, and the introduction of your products and our own advertising would be less effective.

We thank you again for giving us this opportunity of acting as your agency and are looking forward to your favorable reply.

Yours faithfully,

Jan P. Syse

Letter 14-6 (Entrust a customer with sole agency)

Dear Sirs,

Thank you very much for your message of February 5 agreeing to act as a sole agent for marketing our goods in Norway. We have approved your proposal after careful consideration and decided to entrust you with the sole agency for our porcelain wares in the territory of Norway.

We have enclosed a draft of the agency agreement. Would you please review it and send us your comments or suggestions on the wording, detailed terms and conditions? A formal agreement will then be drawn up and copies sent for your signature.[12]

We would like to send you our latest catalogue in the two languages of French and English, and 5 pieces of porcelain vases as samples.

We look forward to doing business with you and much appreciate your cooperation and assistance.

Yours faithfully,

Bruce Du

Unit 14　Agency

 Letter 14-7（**Reply to request for renewal of an agency**）

Dear Sirs,

Thank you very much for your message informing us of your decision to prolong our sole agency agreement for one year.

The record of transactions shows a large increase in turnover. It is impossible to achieve such a great success in the sales of our products in Norway without your endeavors. Thanks to your effective sales promotion activities, our porcelain products now occupy 20% of the market share in your country.

We are pleased to prolong the sole agency agreement for one year, from January 1, 2015 to December 31, 2015. We hope to further enhance our happy cooperation relationship.

Yours faithfully,

Bruce Du

 Letter 14-8（**Termination of an agency relation**）

Dear Sirs,

After careful consideration of our operation, we think that it would be in our best interest to change our marketing approach in Sweden. We must inform you with great regret that our sole agency agreement with you will be terminated, effective November 23, 2015.[13]

As shown in the latest sales report, our share in the Sweden porcelain market has dropped from 15% at the end of 2014 down to 6% at the end of October this year. We think the volume of sales in Sweden does not justify continuing this agreement.

We would like to point out that you may continue to purchase porcelain wares from us at standard prices, and wish to thank you for your endeavors in the last two years.

Yours faithfully,

Ross Liang

Letter 14-9 (Amendments to an agency agreement)

Dear Sirs,

Thank you very much for sending us your agency agreement draft.

Generally, we are pleased to accept your draft and hope to expand the sales of your products. We are ready to place orders, but first we would like to request that you add the following two terms to the agency agreement.

Advertising and Publicity Expenses:
Party B shall bear all expenses for advertising and publicity within the Norway territory in the duration of this agreement and submit to Party A all drafts and/or drawings intended for such purposes for prior approval.[14]

Confirmation of Orders:
The quantities, prices and dates of shipment concerning the commodity stated in this agreement shall be confirmed in each transaction, the particulars of which will be shown in Party A's S/C.

We hope this proposal is reasonable and look forward to a good business relationship.

Yours faithfully,

Jan P. Syse

Words and Vocabulary

convenient	a.	便利的,方便的
economical	a.	节约的,经济的
agency	n.	代理
representative	n.	代表
subcontractor	n.	转包商,次承包者
empower	v.	授权,使能够
principal	n.	(经纪人或代理人所代表的)委托人

Unit 14　Agency

prominent	a.	卓越的，显著的，突出的
sufficient	a.	充足的，充裕的
designate	v.	指定
territory	n.	（代理）区域
connections	n.	联系，关系
spirit	n.	烈酒
reliability	n.	可靠，可靠性，信誉
reference	n.	证明人
integrity	n.	完整，完全，商业信誉
well-established	a.	有影响的
expiration	n.	终止
turnover	n.	流通量，营业额
justify	v.	证明……是正确的
marketability	n.	可销售性
endeavor	v.	努力，热情
enhance	v.	完善，提高
effective	a.	生效的，有效的
amendment	n.	修订，修改
submit	v.	提交
prior	a.	优先的，在前的
approval	n.	同意

with great regret	遗憾地
at standard prices	正常价格
agreement draft	协议草案
advertising and publicity expenses	广告宣传费用
non-exclusive/general agent	一般代理
financial soundness	财务状况良好
market share	市场份额
duration of the agency	代理期限
range of products	产品范围
distributing channels	分销渠道
financial standing	财务状况
confirmation of order	订单确认

Notes

1. A foreign agent is well familiar with the local business environment, and knows clearly what goods are needed and what prices are the best in the local market, therefore, it may be convenient and economical for a company to do business through agencies. 国外代理熟悉当地的商业环境，了解当地市场的需求和价格，因此通过代理进行贸易对公司来说是比较方便和经济的。

2. An agency is an organization, especially a company, acting as the representative, agent, or subcontractor of a person or another company. 代理是指某一组织，主要是公司，以某人或另外一家公司代表、代理或次承包商的身份从事活动。
   本句中"act as"的意思是"担任，担当"。

3. ... the principal enters into relations with the customers abroad by the agent who is on behalf of the principal but is not his employee. ……委托人通过代理同国外顾客建立联系，代理代表委托人但并不是他的雇员。
   本句中"on behalf of"的意思是"代表"。

4. The non-exclusive agency, also called the general agent, is a firm or a person who acts under instructions from his principal to sell or buy on the best terms obtainable and who may sell or buy the competitors' goods. 一般代理是指公司或个人按照委托人的指令以最好的条件进行买卖，代理可以同时买卖委托人竞争对手的商品。
   本句中的"on the best terms"意思是"以最好的条件"；"obtainable"是后置定语，修饰"terms"。

5. ... make inquires into the qualifications, experiences and other necessary information of the agent candidates, such as the reliability and financial soundness, their market connections and sales channels... ……查询代理候选人的资质、经验和其他必要信息，如可靠性、财务状况、市场网络和销售渠道等……
   本句中的"market connections"意思是"市场网络"。

6. A formal agreement on agency may include the following items: the nature and duration of the agency, the territory to be covered, the duties of the parties concerned, the method of purchase and sale, and the commission for the agency. 正式的代理协议包括以下条款：代理性质和期限、代理区域、双方义务、买卖方式和佣金等。
   本句中的"duration"意思是"期限，有效期"。

7. We understand you specialize on porcelain products and are writing to ask if you would be interested in marketing our products in your country on a commission basis. 我们知道贵方专门经营陶瓷产品，不知有没有兴趣以提取佣金的方式在贵国销售我们的产品。

8. We have better knowledge of the market here and good and effective distributing channels. 我们熟悉当地市场，拥有良好有效的分销渠道。

本句中的"have better knowledge of"意思是"对……更熟悉，更了解"。

9. They will offer you the first-class references that prove us agents of high integrity.
   他们将会向您提供一流的证明，证明我们是具有良好商业信誉的代理。

10. The agency agreement has been drawn up for a duration of one year, automatically renewable on expiration for a similar period unless a written notice is given the contrary. 代理协议初定为1年，到期后自动延续1年，除非有相反意愿的书面通知。
    本句中的"draw up"意思是"起草，草拟"。

11. We appreciate your offering, but we decided not to commit ourselves at this stage when the record of transactions shows only a moderate volume of business.　感谢贵公司的提议，但目前交易记录显示贸易额并不大，因此我们歉难答应贵方的代理请求。
    本句中的"at this stage"意思是"现阶段"。

12. A formal agreement will then be drawn up and copies sent for your signature.
    我们将起草正式协议，并将副本寄给贵方签字。

13. We must inform you with great regret that our sole agency agreement with you will be terminated, effective November 23, 2015.　很遗憾地通知贵方，我方将终止我们之间的独家代理协议，并于2015年11月23日生效。

14. Party B shall bear all expenses for advertising and publicity within the Norway territory in the duration of this Agreement and submit to Party A all drafts and/or drawings intended for such purposes for prior approval.　乙方在本协议有效期内承担在挪威境内的所有广告宣传费用，并根据之前承诺向甲方提交所有为此目的服务的草案和（或）图纸。
    本句中"bear expenses"的意思是"承担费用"，"prior approval"的意思是"先前的承诺"。

Sentence Menu

1. Ask to be an agent

(1) This is to inform that we are acting as agents on commission basis. We shall be pleased if you could accord us exclusive selling rights for your ... in ...

(2) We have already represented several other manufacturers and trust you will allow us to give you similar services.

(3) We would like to ask to be the exclusive agent to handle your ... in the territory of ...

(4) We have good knowledge of the local market and are confident that we can expand your business here.

(5) I wonder whether your company is presented in our country.

(6) Considering we have a bright prospect for the sales of your new products, we should like to act as your agent in the market here in this line of business.

(7) We wish to handle as an agent the goods you are exporting now, because we are

commanding an extensive domestic market in this line.

(8) We have been dealing with you in this line for many years and have offices or representatives in all major cities and towns in this country, therefore, we are confident that our capability will justify your appointing us as your exclusive agent.

(9) In case you are interested in a representative in the territory of ..., we believe we can do a substantial job for you.

2. Reply to a request for an agency

(1) We thank you for you letter offering your services and would like to discuss the possibility of an agency with you.

(2) Please let us be notified whether you now represent any manufacturers in the same line.

(3) As our sole agent, you should undertake neither to sell any products of any other manufacturers in the same line nor re-export our products to any other areas outside ...

(4) We inform you with great regret that our agency representation has been taken over by someone else in ...

(5) As regards the matter of exclusive agency, we are not yet prepared to consider it now. We shall revert to it when business has developed to our mutual satisfaction.

(6) We appreciate your offer to help market our products in ..., but I have to point out that we have never conducted any agency agreement with your company.

(7) Our agency in your district has been vacant and we can appoint you for this position.

(8) After careful consideration, we have decided to appoint you as our agent for the territory of ... on the terms and conditions agreed with you.

(9) In view of your past efforts in pushing the sales of our products, we have decided to accept your proposal and appoint you as our sole agent.

(10) We appreciate your suggestion that you sell our goods on an exclusive basis, but we would like to know the approximate quantity you may sell in the year to come.

(11) We are prepared to appoint you as our agent for your district on a ...% commission basis, which will be remitted to you every three months after our receipt of the payments. We will pay, against the relative invoices, the advertising expenses incurred to you for the promotion of sales of our products.

3. Reply to being offered an agency

(1) Thank you for your offering us the agency in ... for your products and appreciate the confidence you have placed in us.

(2) We are pleased that you are prepared to appoint us as your sole agent for your products.

(3) We hope that we will double our efforts to build a large turnover so as to justify a close arrangement like sole agency.

(4) As your agency, we will make great efforts to push the sales of your products.

(5) I am willing to accept your offer to act as your sales agency.

4. Terminate an agency

(1) With considerable regret, we must inform you that effective ... (specific date), our exclusive agent agreement with you will be terminated.

(2) I am afraid we cannot agree to appoint you as our sole agent because the annual turnover you promise is too low.

(3) We have noticed that in canvassing for orders, you have more than once exceeded the limit of your district.

(4) We regret to inform you that our agency representation has taken over by someone else.

(5) After careful consideration of our operation, we think that it would be in our best interest to change our marketing approach in ...

I Put the following terms or phrases from English into Chinese or vice versa.

1. turnover
2. principal
3. sole agent
4. business integrity
5. advertising and publicity expenses
6. entrust ... with exclusive agency
7. 终止代理协议
8. 交易记录
9. 代理协议草案
10. 书面通知
11. 互利贸易
12. 代理区域

II Fill in the blanks of the following letter with the words given below, and change the form when necessary.

approve, entrust, message, duration, territory, notice, enclose, review, careful, renew

Dear Sirs,

Thank you for your _____ of February 3 asking to be our sole agent. After _____ consideration, we decided to _____ you with the sole agency for our products in the _____ of Portugal.

The agency agreement has been drawn up for the _____ of one year, automatically _____ on expiration for a similar period unless _____ is given to the contrary.

_____ is a copy of the draft. Please _____ the provisions and advise us whether they meet with you _____.

We are looking forward to your reply.

Yours faithfully,

Alfred Liu

III **Complete the following sentences with the Chinese given in the brackets.**

1. The question of agency is _____（正在考虑之中）, and we hope that _____（贵方将继续努力提高我方产品的销售）。
2. Commission rate will be increased _____（与贵方的销售数量成比例）。
3. Once an agency agreement is concluded, _____（委托方和代理方都将承担一定的义务）。
4. The agency must not divulge confidential material or information to a third party _____ _____（在代理期间和之后）。
5. If the present trend continues, Showner will have _____（将把市场份额提高到30%）by the end of the year.
6. As an exclusive agent of yours, I have every reason to _____（使委托人知晓我最近做的调查）。
7. This agency agreement is entered into between the parties concerned _____ （在平等互利的基础上按照以下双方同意的条款进行贸易）。

IV **Translate the following letter into English.**

敬启者：

谢谢贵方2月4日的来函，自荐担任我方在摩洛哥的代理。

鉴于目前交易额不大，我们认为考虑代理事宜为时尚早，双方有必要再试行合作一段时间，看交易情况如何，这对你我双方更为有益。贵公司应该进一步增加营业额，以便证明可以签订代理协议。

相信你方能够理解我方看法，共同努力以促进彼此之间愉快的合作关系。

敬上

V Writing practice.

Situational Writing 1

Write a letter with the following given particulars.

- 自荐担任独家代理，销售数码相机。
- 对本地市场了如指掌。
- 拥有良好的分销和零售渠道。
- 当地市场对所代理产品的需求持续增长。

Situational Writing 2

Suppose you are working for a US medical equipment company. You received a claim from your agent in the mainland of China complaining that your agent in Hong Kong exceeded the limit of their district to canvass for orders in Beijing and Guangdong province. You made an investigation and found that it was true. **You are requested to write a letter to the agent in Hong Kong to terminate the agency agreement.**

Unit 15

Contracts
合　同

A contract is an agreement that defines a relationship between one or more parties, and the essence of a contract is the mutual understanding reached by two parties who hold adverse positions against each other. Once signed, a contract is enforceable by law. Any party that fails to fulfill its contract obligations may be ordered to make compensation.

Contracts can be formal and informal. For an informal contract, writing is not always necessary. A spoken word will do. But formal contracts require certain formalities. They are mostly made for large or important details. They should be detailed and specific, stating all terms and conditions agreed upon by the parties and listing the rights and obligations of the two parties and all matters concerning the transaction.

15.1 Types of Business Contracts

1. Form-style Contract and Clause-style Contract

The form-style contract is generally the standard contract, which is printed in advance with some blanks left for future signature. Compared with the formal-style contract, the clause-style contract is more complex and detailed. The terms and conditions are concretely stated with substantial sub-clauses.

2. In Terms of Function and Contents

1) Sales contract and purchase contract

The sales contract is an agreement between the seller and the buyer. When the contract is made by the seller, it is called a sales contract, when made by the buyer, a purchase contract. A sales or purchase confirmation is less detailed than a contract, covering only the essential terms of the transaction. It is usually used for smaller deals or between familiar trade partners. A sales contract usually contains:

(1) information about the offeror;

(2) name and address of offeree;
(3) information on the goods to be sold or bought, such as specification, quantity, and price, etc;
(4) payment conditions;
(5) transport conditions; which party will be responsible for obtaining the necessary licenses and for the customs formalities;
(6) insurance conditions;
(7) time and place of delivery;
(8) inspection, force majeure;
(9) the law applicable to the contract;
(10) means for arbitration or settlement of any disputes;
(11) any other points the offeror considers relevant to the proposed contract.

Under a sales contract, the seller must have to deliver the goods, hand over relevant documents, such as the bill of lading, commercial invoice, certificate of origins and etc as required by the contract. As for the buyer, he must make payments of the goods and take delivery of them as stipulated in the contract.

2) Counter-trade contract

Counter-trade contracts include barter, switch, and offset, etc. A barter contract is a contract covering the simple exchange of goods. A switch contract covers the purchase of goods in a non-convertible currency and their sales in a convertible currency. But offset contract means that an exporter buys goods from a market and makes a counter-balancing sale to the market.

3) Leasing contract

Under a leasing contract, the owner of a property, or leaser, gives the exclusive right of the use of that property to someone else, the lessee

4) Engineering contract

Engineering contracts generally include construction contract and contracts for delivery. Construction contracts cover the construction of buildings or other high-rise structures, roads, bridges, tunnels and other civil works. Contracts for delivery refer to the engineering contracts that provide for the delivery of either mechanical or electronic equipment or both.

5) Foreign investment and joint venture agreement

Agreements covering foreign investments usually consist of several inter-related contracts. The main contract may be a joint venture agreement. The other agreements may cover such matters as the set-up of a new company, transfer of technology and other areas essential to the implementation of the main contract.

6) Transfer of technology agreement

It is generally called licensing agreements. Under the agreement, the owner of a trademark of patent allows someone to use it. Licensing agreement often forms part of joint venture agreements and sometimes of engineering agreements

15.2 Components of a Business Contract

A contract should contain the following items in the order of the following: the title, contract proper, the signature and attached schedules, if there is any.

1. The Title

The type of the contract is indicated in the title such as Sales Contract, Purchase Contract, Consignment Contract, etc. The number of the contract and the date are given below the title to the right side.

2. The Contract Proper

This part includes: ① the full name address of the buyer and the seller; ② the commodities involved including quantity, quality, specifications, packing, etc; ③ all the terms and conditions agreed upon such as the price, total amount, terms of payment, transportation, insurance etc; ④ indication of the number of original copies of the contract, the languages used, the term of validity and possible extension of the contract.

3. The Signature

The signature of the contracting parties indicating their status as the seller or the buyer.

4. The Stipulations on the Back of the Contract

They are constituent parts of the contract and are equally binding upon the contracting parties. These may include the shipping documents required, force majeure, arbitration, claims etc.

15.3 Language and Stylistics Features

The formal international sales contract, strictly speaking, is one of the legal documents. It has many features of the legal English.

1. Lexical

1) Employment of archaic words and phrases

In order to render the contract formal and dignified, composers, usually lawyers, often employ words and phrases that are unique to this variety. In our daily trade practice, we often come across archaic words like *thereafter*, *thereby*, *heretofore*, *hereinabove* and etc. These all present a degree of formality.

2) Preference for lexical repetition to pronoun reference

In order to achieve exactness of reference, leaving no loopholes whatsoever, contract composers tend to use lexical repetition as the formal device to link their long and self-contained sentences. Repetition of the same exact word or phrase not only occurs between sentences, but also between different parts within the same sentences. On the other way round, preference for pronoun is rare. Actually in legal documents, almost no pronoun is used unless it is unmistakably clear. Repetition within the same sentence is remarkably unique in this variety. Look at the following example:

Having examined the conditions of contract specifications, drawings and bill of quantities for the execution of the abovementioned works, we the undersigned, offer to execute and complete such works in conformity with the conditions of contract, specification, drawings and bill of quantities.

3) Special use of common words

Like all other specialists who have built a technical vocabulary for themselves, the professional composers of contracts, who are profound in law and business, also have a set of technical words at their disposal.

Common words used in such a special way and the technical terms help to mark out the contract is belonging to the field of both legal and business English, which also shows the composers' effort to guard against any disputable man-in-street understanding of the respective meanings and avoid any possible misinterpretation.[1]

4) Heavy use of *and*, *or* and *and/or*

So when the composer prepares a contract, he tries to cover everything and take every detail and condition into account. The clause, with the use of *and/or*, can clearly cover every circumstance that may happen, which helps to avoid any disputes beforehand. Look at the special use of *and/or* in the following samples:

The prices mentioned herein are all based upon the current rate freight and/or war and marine insurance premium.

Any increase in freight and/or insurance premium rate at the time of shipment shall be for BUYERS' risk and account.

The clause, with the use of *and/or*, clearly covers every circumstance that may happen, which helps to avoid any disputes beforehand and has guaranteed the SELLERS' interests.

2. Grammatical

1) Wide use of statement-type sentences

As is the nature of legal documents, most of the sentences of a contract are in the form of statements with no questions. Occasionally a command tone is used at the beginning or the end of the contract. A large number of sentences are of the structure SPO(C)A or ASPOC. We may tell this from the following insurance clause.

S SELLERS
P shall arrange
O marine insurance covering WA plus TPND and war risk for 110% of the invoice value
P and provide for
C if any
O claim, payable in New York in US currency

In this sentence, there's an adverbial introduced by *if any*.

The claim clause, however, is different from the above one.

A In any event
S SELLERS
P shall be responsible for
O damages that may result from the use of the goods or for consequential or special damages, or for any amount in excess of the invoice value of the defective goods.

Conditional clauses introduced by *if*, *provided that*, *in the event*, etc. are many in this variety. Attention should be paid to the unusual positioning of adverbials in this variety of English. Normally adverbials are not placed between a transitive verb and its objects, but adverbials often come before the object in legal English. In formal contracts, we often come across sentences as follows:

To pay on behalf of . . . all sums

A proposal to effect with the society an assurance . . .[2]

No doubt the idea is given emphasis to the adverbials or to avoid any possible ambiguity.

2) Simple present tense

The composer uses the simple present tense when he makes a contract. The past consideration is not consideration. The consideration (called conditions in the Civil Law System) and the obligation of both parties are realized at present or in the future, therefore using the simple present tense is the general rule for making contracts.

3) Use of simpler verbal groups

Compared with nominal groups, verbal groups in legal documents are structured simple. Quite a number of verbs are of the type "modal auxiliary (often *shall*) + be + participle" or "modal auxiliary (often *shall* or *may*) + be or do". *Shall* is invariably used to express obligation or certainty.

4) Long sentences

The composer of a formal contract tends to employ complex sentences with an array of subordinating devices for it is believed that each legal sentence is a self-contained unit and conveys all the sense that has to be conveyed. The front page of Sample 2 is of only one sentence but contains 72 words and A sentence under the FORCE MAJEURE clause has as many as 70 words.

3. Stylistic

1) Being concise and straightforward

Contracts are to be scrutinized not only by the parties concerned but also by lawyers when necessary, so whoever draws up a contract is constantly and inescapably concerned with the special kind of meaning that he or she is called upon to produce. He or she must meet the demands to be precise and exact, to avoid ambiguity and the possibilities of misinterpretation so as to conform to the linguistic dictates of the law. Therefore, meticulous way of expression is adopted to achieve exactness of reference lest there arise anything disputable concerning the stipulations on the right and obligations. Still let's look at the following sample:

Any disputes, controversies or difference which may arise between the parties, out of, or in relation to, or in connection with the contract[3] . . .

By such wording, every circumstance that may cause disputes, controversies, or differences has been taken into consideration and placed under stipulation.

2) Clarity

The sales letter is closely organized and full of specific details. The composer identifies exactly what the problem is and what he would like to do. There is also no ambiguous phrase: the message is clear on the first brief reading. All these make the reader never have to puzzle out his meaning and have no unanswered questions after reading the letter.

15.4 Layout

1. Use of Different Types

The purpose of this kind of arrangement is to make the main points be caught easily, because the use of different types is a weapon of drawing the reader's attention to the particular important places in a contract.

2. Particular Arrangement of Blocks

The blocks of print are clear with white space between them and with indentations and/or numbers (or letters) at the beginning of paragraphs or clauses that are subordinate to the foregoing paragraph. All these are evidently efforts to give the content a good organization and make its internal relations clear. Some of the long sentence are broken up by spaces to mark out certain important points.

3. Limited Range of Punctuation

The most characteristic phenomenon of some old form of legal documents is perhaps the dearth of punctuation. Many of them are either unpunctuated or punctuated only with a final period or a colon. The idea is to avoid any possible forgery—either addition or deletion.

Today, however, the tendency is to employ a limited range of punctuation marks as a useful guide to grammatical structure. The most frequently used are commas and periods, but we also find many colons and semicolons appear in documents. Together with numbers (letters) and block arrangement, they make the clauses of the contract much easier to refer to. For example:

Any disputes, controversies or difference which may arise between the parties, out of, or in relation to, or in connection with the contract.[3]

15.5 Writing Steps

Step 1 Ascertaining Basic Documents

Many documents are expected to be drafted before a contract is finally completed, and these basic documents generally include the letters of inquiry, offer and counteroffer, acceptance, minutes of talks and memorandums.

Step 2　Familiarizing Contract Formats

Business contracts can be classified into various categories, and the parties should choose the right one and the right format. The following are some examples employed often in international business: contracts for international sale of goods, contracts for international technology transfer, contracts for international engineering projects, contracts for foreign labor services, contracts for international leasing affairs, contracts for credits and loans, and contracts for international build-operate-transfer (BOT).

Step 3　Standardizing the Structure

A standardized contract is usually made up of a preamble, main body and a section of final clauses. The preamble displays the corporate or personal names of the parties, their nationalities, principal places of business or residential addresses and the date and place for signing of the contract. The main body covers the various rights and obligations of the parties concerned, while languages in which the contract is to be written, validity of the contract, and signature are put in the section of the final clauses.

Step 4　Clarifying the Specific Conditions and Terms

Conditions in a contract are designed to specify a requirement or prerequisite, namely, to state a requirement that must be fulfilled, or to make something dependent on a requirement, while terms are the particular requirements laid down formally in an agreement or contract, or proposed by one side when negotiating an agreement.

To clarify the specific conditions and terms, the producer of a contract may study some sample forms first and these sample forms are expected to be similar to the situation. The study of such samples can help alert the producer to issues not considered. In addition, these samples provide good samples of language for the preparation of the contract.

However, the form chosen may not be applicable to the situation or it is drafted for the benefit of the wrong side, so the drafter has to revise the specific conditions and terms, and create new articles to guarantee the interests of his organization.

Step 5　Referring to International Conventions and Practices

Various international conventions and practices have been established in international trade in the last decades and these conventions and practices can greatly facilitate transactions across different countries and therefore are followed by many individuals and organizations. The drafter should make sure if our country has signed or approved those conventions, and then refer to those conventions and practices to avoid cheats and risks. The most popular international conventions and practices in foreign trade are the United Nations Convention on International Sales of Goods (CISG) and Incoterms 2010.

Step 6　Standardizing the Language

The last step is to review the draft contract, focusing on the language. The drafter should review every word to polish any expression that is ambiguous or that may incur unnecessary disputes. When standardizing the language, the drafter can also refer to relevant sample forms and borrow their words, phrases, and structures.

Sample 1 A Sales Confirmation

SHANGHAI TEXTILES TRADING CO., LTD.

H. Woods & Co., Ltd. September 6, 2015
Nesson House, Newell Street
Birmingham B15 3EL
United Kingdom

SALES CONFIRMATION

We confirm having sold to you the following merchandise on terms and conditions set forth below:

Article: Printed Cotton Sheeting
Specification: #2006
  30's × 30's, 68 × 60, 35/36" in width
  abt. 40 yds, per piece
Quality: as per our sample submitted on August 25, 2015
Quantity: 50,000 yd
Price: US$0.76 per yd, CIF Birmingham
Amount: US$38,000.00
Packing: in export standard bales packing
Shipment: during November/December, 2015
Partial shipment to be allowed
Destination: Birmingham, United Kingdom
Payment: draft at sight under an irrevocable letter of credit to be opened by the end of October 2015
Insurance: against WPA plus war for 110% of Invoice Value
Remarks: (1) Your commission 3% on FOB value has been included in the above price.
  (2) Please open L/C advising through Bank of China.

Accepted by: Yours faithfully,
 (Buyer) SHANGHAI TEXTILES TRADING CO., LTD.

Sample 2　A Sales Contract

Contract

Seller：

Address：

Buyer：

Address：

双方同意按下列条款由卖方出售，买方买进下列货物：

The Seller agrees to sell and the Buyer agrees to buy the undermentioned goods on the terms and conditions stated below：

（1）货物名称、规格、包装及唛头 Name of Commodity, Specifications, Packing Terms and Shipping Marks	（2）数量 Quantity	（3）单价 Unit Price	（4）总值 Total Value
检验：以中国商品检验局出具的品质重量证书作为付款依据。 Inspection：The certificates of quality and weight issued by the China Commodity Inspection Bureau are to be taken as the basis for effecting payment.	卖方有权在＿＿＿％内多装或少装 Shipment ＿＿＿％ more or less at Seller's option		

（5）装运期限：

Time of Shipment：

（6）装运口岸：

Port of Loading：

（7）目的口岸：

Por t of Destination：

（8）保险：由卖方按发票金额110%投保

Insurance：To be effected by the sellers for 110% of invoice value covering

（9）付款条件：凭保兑的、不可撤销的、可转让的、可分割的即期信用证在中国见单付款。信用证以卖方为受益人，并允许分批装运和转船，该信用证必须在装运月＿＿＿天前开到卖方，并在装船后在上述转船港继续有效15天，否则卖方无需通知即有权取消本销售合同，并向买方索赔因此而发生的一切损失。

Terms of Payment：By confirmed, irrevocable, transferable and divisible letter of credit in favor of the Seller payable at sight against presentation of shipping documents in China, with partial shipments and transshipment allowed. The covering letter of credit must reach the Seller ＿＿＿ days before the contracted month of shipment and remain valid in the above loading port until the 15th day after shipment, failing which the Seller reserve the rights to cancel the contract without further notice and to claim against the Buyer for any loss resulting there from.

（10）单据：卖方应向议付银行提供已装船清洁提单、发票、中国商品检验局或工厂出具的品质证明、中国商品检验局出具的数/重量鉴定书；如果本合同按 CIF 条件，应再提供可转让的保险单或保险凭证。

Documents: The Seller shall present the negotiating bank clean on board bill of lading, invoice, quality certificate issued by the China Commodity Inspection Bureau or the manufacturers, survey report on quantity/weight issued by the China Commodity Inspection Bureau, and transferable insurance policy or insurance certificate when this contract is made on CIF basis.

（11）装运条件：装运船只由卖方安排，允许分批装运并允许转船。卖方于货物装船后，应将合同号码、品名、数量、船名、装船日期以电报通知对方。

Terms of Shipment: The carrying vessel shall be provided by the Seller. Partial shipments and transshipment are allowed. After loading is completed, the Seller shall notify the Buyer by cable of the contract number, name of commodity, quantity, name of the carrying vessel and date of shipment.

（12）品质与数量、重量的异议与索赔：货到目的口岸后，买方如发现货物品质及/或数量/重量与合同规定不符，除属于保险公司及/或船公司的责任外，买方可以凭双方同意的检验机构出具的检验证书向卖方提出异议。品质异议须于货到目的口岸之日起 30 天内提出，数量/重量异议须于货到目的口岸之日起 15 天内提出。卖方应于收到异议后 30 天内答复买方。

Quality and/or Quantity/Weight Discrepancy and Claim: In case the quality and/or quantity/weight are found by the Buyer to be not in conformity with the contract after the arrival of the goods at the port of destination, the Buyer may lodge claim with the seller supported by the survey report issued by an inspection organization agreed upon by both parties, with the exception, however, of those claims for which the insurance company and/or the shipping company are to be held responsible. Claim for quality discrepancy should be filed by the Buyer within 30 days after the arrival of the goods at the port of destination, while claim for quantity/weight discrepancy should be filed by the buyer within 15 days after the arrival of the goods at the port of destination. The Seller shall, within 30 days after receipt of the notification of the claim, send reply to the Buyer.

（13）人力不可抗拒：由于人力不可抗拒事故，使卖方不能在本合同规定期限内交货或者不能交货，卖方不负责任。但卖方必须立即以电报通知买方。如买方提出要求，卖方应以挂号函向买方提供由中国国际贸易促进会或有关机构出具的发生事故的证明文件。

Force Majeure: In case of force majeure, the Seller shall not be held responsible for late delivery or non-delivery of the goods, but shall notify the buyers by cable. The Seller shall deliver to the Buyer by registered mail, if so requested by the Buyer, a certificate issued by the China Council for the Promotion of International Trade and/or competent authorities.

（14）仲裁：凡因执行本合同或与本合同有关事项所发生的一切争执，应由双方通过友好的方式协商解决。如果不能取得协议时，则在被告国家根据被告仲裁机构的仲裁程序进行仲裁。仲裁决定是终局的，对双方具有同等的约束力。仲裁费用除非仲裁机构另有决定外，均由败诉一方负担。

Arbitration: All disputes in connection with this contract or the execution thereof shall be settled by negotiation between two parties. If no settlement can be reached, the case in dispute shall then be submitted for arbitration in the country of defendant in accordance with the arbitration regulations of the arbitration organization of the defendant country. The decision made by the arbitration organization shall be taken as final and binding upon both parties. The arbitration expenses shall be borne by the losing party unless otherwise awarded by the arbitration organization.

（15）备注：
Remarks：

卖方： 买方：
Sellers： Buyers：

 Sample 3 Conditions of Contract for EPC/Turnkey Projects（Extracts）

4 Contractors

4.1 Contractor's General Obligations

The contractor shall design, execute and complete, the works in accordance with the contract, and shall remedy any defects in the works. When completed, the works shall be fit for the purpose for which the works are intended as defined in the contract.

The contractor shall provide the plant and contractor's documents specified in the contract, and all the contractor's personnel, goods, consumables and other goods and services, whether of a temporary nature, required in and for this design, execution, completion and remedying of defects.

The works shall include any work which is necessary to satisfy the Employer's requirements, or is implied by the contract, and all works which (although not mentioned in the contract) are necessary for stability or for the completion, or safe and proper operation, of the works.

The contractor shall be responsible for all the adequacy, stability and safety of all site operations, of all methods of construction and of all the works.

The contractor shall, whenever required by the employer, submit details of the arrangements and methods which the contractor proposes to adopt for the execution of the works. No significant alteration to these arrangements and methods shall be made without this having previously been notified to the Employer.

4.2 Performance Security

The contractor shall obtain (at his cost) a performance security for proper performance, in the amount and currencies stated in the particular conditions. If an amount is not stated in the particular conditions, this sub-clause shall not apply.

The contractor shall deliver the performance security to the employer within 28 days after both parties have signed the contract agreement. The performance security shall be issued by an entity and from within a country (or other jurisdiction) approved by the employer, and shall be in the form annexed to the particular conditions or in another form approved by the employer.

The contractor shall ensure that the performance security is valid and enforceable until the contractor has executed and completed the works and remedied any defects. If the terms of the performance security specify its expiry date, and the contractor has not become entitled to receive the performance certificate by the date 28 days prior to the expiry date, the contractor shall extend the validity of the performance security until the works have been completed and any defects have been remedied.

The employer shall not make a claim under the performance security, except for amounts to which the employer is entitled under the contract in the event of:

(A) Failure by the contractor to extend the validity of the performance security as described in the preceding paragraph, in which event the employer may claim the full amount of the performance security,

(B) Failure by the contractor to pay the employer an amount due, as either agreed by the contractor or determined under sub-clause 2.5 [Employer's Claims] or clause 20 [Claims, Disputes and Arbitration], within 42 days after this agreement or determination,

(C) Failure by the contractor to remedy a default within 42 days after receiving the employer's notice requiring the default to be remedied, or

(D) Circumstances which entitle the employer to termination under sub-clauses 15.2 [Termination by Employer], irrespective of whether notice of termination has been given.

The employer shall indemnify and hold the contractor harmless against and from all damages, losses and expenses (including legal fees and expenses) resulting from a claim under the performance security to the extent to which the employer was not entitled to make the claim.

The employers shall return the performance security to the contractor within 21 days after the contractor has become entitled to receive the performance certificate.

4.3 Contractor's Representative

The contractor shall appoint the contractor representative, and awarded him with all the necessary rights that he needs to act on behalf of the contract.

Unless the contractor's representative is named in the contract, the contractor shall, prior to the commencement date, submit to the employer for consent the name and particulars of the person the contractor proposes to appoint as contractor's representative. If consent is withheld or subsequently revoked, or if the appointed person fails to act as contractor's representative, the contractor shall similarly submit the name and particulars of another suitable person for such appointment.

The contractor shall not, without the prior consent of the employer, revoke the appointment of the contractor's representative or appoint a replacement.

The contractor's representative may delegate any powers, functions and authority to any competent person, and may at any time revoke the delegation. Any delegation or revocation shall not take effect until the employer has received prior notice signed by the contractor's representative, naming the person and specifying the powers, functions and authority being delegated or revoked.

The contractor's representative and all these personnel shall be fluent in the language for communication defined in sub-Clause 1.4 [Law and Language].

4.4 Subcontractors

The contractor shall not subcontract the whole of the works.

The contractor shall be responsible for the acts or defaults of any subcontractor, his agents or employees, as if they were the acts or defaults of the contractor. Where specified in the particular conditions, the contractor shall give the employer not less than 28 days' notice of:

(A) The intended appointment of the subcontractor, with detailed particulars which shall include his relevant experience,

(B) The intended commencement of the subcontractor's work, and

(C) The intended commencement of the subcontractor's work on the site.

4.5 Nominated Subcontractors

In this sub-clause, the "nominated subcontractor" refers to the subcontractor whom the employer, under Clause 13 [Variations and Adjustments], instructs the contractor to employ as a subcontractor. The Contractor shall not be under any obligation to employ a nominated subcontractor against whom the contractor raises reasonable objection by notice to the employer as soon as practicable, with supporting particulars.

4.6 Cooperation

Contractor shall, as specified in the contract or as instructed by the employer, allow appropriate opportunities for carrying out work to:

(A) the employer's personnel,

(b) any other contractors employed by the employer, and

(c) the personnel of any legally constituted public authorities, who may be employed in the execution on or near the site of any work not included in the contract.

Any such instruction shall constitute a variation if and to extent that it causes the contractor to incur cost in an amount which was not reasonably foreseeable by an experienced contractor by the date for submission of the tender. Services for these personnel and other contractors may include the use of contractor's equipment temporary works or access arrangements which are the responsibility of the contractor.

The contractor shall be responsible for the construction activities in the field, and shall, co-ordinate his own activities with those of other contractors to the extent (if any) specified in the employer's requirements.

If under the contract, employers are required to give to the contractor the possession of any foundation, structure, plant or means of access in accordance with contractor's documents, the contractor shall submit such documents to the employer in the time and manner stated in the employer's requirements.

4.7 Setting Out

The contractor shall set out the works in relation to original points, lines and levels of reference specified in the contract. The contractor shall be responsible for the correct positioning of all parts of the works, and shall rectify any error in the positions, levels, dimensions or alignment of the works.

4.8 Safety Procedures

Contractor shall:

(A) comply with all applicable safety rules,

(B) take care of the safety of all persons entitled to be on the site,

Use reasonable efforts to keep the site and works clear of unnecessary obstruction so as to avoid danger to these persons,

(D) provide fencing, lighting, guarding and watching of the works until completion and taking over under Clause10 [Employer Receives] and,

(E) provide any temporary works (including roadways, footways, guards and fences, etc.) which may be necessary, because of the execution of the works, for the use and protection of the public and owners and occupiers of adjacent land.

4.9 Quality Assurance

The Contractor shall establish a quality assurance system to demonstrate compliance with contract requirements. The system should be in accordance with the detailed provisions of the contract. Employers shall be entitled to audit any aspect of the system.

Details of all procedures and compliance documents shall be submitted to the employer for information before each design and execution stage is commenced. When any document of a technical nature is issued to the employer, evidence of the prior approval by the contractor himself shall be apparent on the document itself.

4.10 Site Data

The employer shall have made available to the contractor for his instruction, prior to the Base Date, all relevant data in the employer's possession on subsurface and hydrological conditions at the site, including environment aspects. The Employer shall similarly make available to the contractor all such data which come into the employer's possession after the base data.

The contractor shall be responsible for the verifying and interpreting all such data. The employer shall have no responsibility for the accuracy, sufficiency or completeness of such data, except as stated in sub-clause 5.1[General Design Responsibility].

Words and Vocabulary

archaic	a.	古老的，古代的，陈旧的
thereafter	ad.	其后，从那时以后
thereby	ad.	因此，从而
heretofore	ad.	直到此时，迄今
hereinabove	ad.	在上文
herein	ad.	于此，在这里
complex	a.	复杂的，合成的
subordinating	a.	连接主句和从句的
adverbial	n.	状语
ambiguity	n.	含糊，不明确
scrutinize	v.	细察
dictate	v.	规定，指示
lexical	a.	词汇的
loophole	n.	漏洞
whatsoever	pron.	无论什么
unmistakably	ad.	明白地
undersign	v.	在……的下面签名，签名于末尾
specification	n.	详述，规格
meticulous	a.	小心翼翼的
indentation	n.	缩排，呈锯齿状，缺口
foregoing	a.	在前的，前述的

Unit 15 Contracts

dearth	n.	缺乏
forgery	n.	伪造物，伪造
preamble	n.	导言
principal	a.	主要的，首要的
validity	n.	有效性，合法性
prerequisite	n.	先决条件
incur	v.	招致
invoice	n.	发票，发票额
provision	n.	规定，条款
contracting parties		签约方
provided that		假如，设若
modal auxiliary		情态动词
bill of quantities		数量清单
technology transfer		技术转让
international leasing affairs		国际租赁业务
foreign labor service		国外劳务服务
credits and loans		信用和贷款
in excess of		超过，超出
force majeure		不可抗力
exclusive right		专有权

Notes

1. ... the composers' effort to guard against any disputable man-in-street understanding of the respective meanings and avoid any possible misinterpretation.　……合同撰写人努力避免任何可能产生争议的大众化理解，以及任何可能的曲解。

2. A proposal to effect with the society an assurance ...　一个向社会保证……的建议

3. Any disputes, controversies or difference which may arise between the parties, out of, or in relation to, or in connection with the contract.　双方因合同或与合同相关的事宜而产生的争议、矛盾或分歧。
   "in connection with" 意为"与……有关"。

4. SELLERS reserve the right to adjust the price mentioned herein, if prior to delivery there is any substantial increase in the cost of raw material or component parts.　交货前如果原材料或零部件价格有任何实质性的增长，卖方保留调整价格的权利。

5. ... in case the merchandise has been prepared and ready for shipment before shipment deadline

but the shipment could not be effected due to any of the above-mentioned causes, BUYERS shall extend the shipping deadline by means of amending relevant L/C or otherwise, upon the request of SELLERS. 如果在装运截止日期前货物已备好，但因上述任何原因而无法启运，买方应，或应卖方请求，通过修改相关信用证延长装运日期。

6. IN WITNESS WHEREOF, the parties have executed this contract in duplicate by their duly authorized representative as on the date first above written. 本合同由双方充分授权的代表于上述日期履行生效，一式两份，以资证明。

7. The Service Partner will provide after-sales services, including site inspection, installation, handing over, maintenance and application training, and warranty and modifications, during the warranty and after-warranty periods upon request of ABC within the defined territory. 在规定区域内，应ABC公司请求，服务合作商在保修期和保修期后提供各种售后服务，包括现场勘查、安装、转交、维护、应用培训、保修和维修等。

8. In case any amount is deducted by ABC according to the provisions contained in this Agreement, the Service Partner shall pay to ABC within [ ] days so as to keep the Performance Bond up to RMB300,000. 如果ABC公司根据本合同规定扣除一定金额，服务合作商应该在[ ]日内支付相应金额以使运营保证金保持在30万元人民币。

9. The Service Partner shall not disclose to any other parties any technical or marketing information (e.g. drawings, internal interfaces, software) of a confidential nature which it may acquire in the course of its cooperation with ABC, and shall also prevent the afore mentioned information from being disclosed to or used by unauthorized persons or parties. 因保密原因，服务合作商不可向其他任何方披露在与ABC公司合作中可能获得的任何技术或营销信息（如图纸、内部界面和软件），同时应该防止未经授权的任何人或组织了解地使用上述信息。

10. Without prejudice to any other remedies available to ABC as provided in other Articles of this Agreement, where the Service Partner fails to perform any of its obligations under this Agreement.... 在服务合作商没有履行本合同的任何义务时，应毫无区别地使用本合同其他条款提供的ABC公司可以获取的任何救济方式。

11. The award of the arbitration tribunal shall be final and binding upon the disputing Parties, and the winning Party may, at the cost and expenses of the losing Party, apply to any court of competent jurisdiction for enforcement of such award. 仲裁结果为最终裁决，对争议双方具有约束力，胜方在败方负担费用的情况下，可向任何有效法院申请执行仲裁裁决。

12. If there is any discrepancy between the Appendices and/or Attachments and any terms and conditions in this Agreement, the terms and conditions in this Agreement shall prevail. 如果附件或附录和本合同条款有任何冲突，以合同条款为准。

13. This Agreement shall be effective as of the date on which the Parties hereto have caused this Agreement to be executed by their duly authorized representatives. 本合同于经充分授权的代表签署之日起生效。

Sentence Menu

(1) We confirm having sold to you the following merchandise on terms and conditions set forth below:

(2) This agreement is made between Party A and Party B in respect of...

(3) This contract is made this 15th day of... by A (hereinafter referred to as "SELLERS"), a corporation having their principal office at..., who agree to sell, and B (hereinafter referred to as "BUYERS"), a corporation having their principal office at..., who agree to buy the following goods on the terms and conditions as below:

(4) To be shipped on or before... subject to acceptable L/C reached SELLERS before..., and partial shipments allowed, transshipment allowed.

(5) SELLERES shall arrange marine insurance covering... for 110% of the invoice value and provide for claim, if any, payable in... in... currency

(6) In the event of any claim arising in respect of any shipment, notice of intention to claim should be given in writing to...

(7) IN WITNESS WHEREOF, the parties have executed this contract in duplicate by their duly authorized representative as on the date first above written.

(8) WHEREAS, A has appointed B as the agent in...

Exercises

1 The following is the main body of a draft of sale contract. You are required to standardize its structure and format, and make it complete. You may invent any information necessary.

1. Names of commodity(ies) and specification(s)
2. Quantity
3. Unit price
4. Amount TOTAL: _____% more or less allowed
5. Packing:
6. Port of Loading:
7. Port of Destination:
8. Shipping Marks:
9. Time of Shipment: Within _____ days after receipt of L/C, allowing transhipment and partial shipment.
10. Terms of Payment: By 100% Confirmed, Irrevocable and Sight Letter of Credit to remain valid

for negotiation in China until the 15th day after shipment.

11. Insurance: Covers all risks and war risks only as per the Clauses of the People's Insurance Company of China for 110% of the invoice value. To be effected by the Buyer.

12. The Buyer shall establish the covering Letter of Credit before _____; failing which, the Seller reserves the right to rescind this Sales Contract without further notice, or to accept whole or any part of this Sales Contract, non-fulfilled by the Buyer of _____ to lodge claim for direct losses sustained, if any.

13. Documents: The Sellers shall present to the negotiating bank, Clean on Board Bill of Lading, Invoice, Quality Certificate issued by the China Commodity Inspection Bureau or the Manufacturers, Survey Report on Quantity/Weight issued by the China Commodity Inspection Bureau, and Transferable Insurance policy or Insurance Certificate when this contract is made on CIF basis.

14. For this contract signed on CIF basis, the premium should be 110% of invoice value. All risks insured should be included within this contract. If the Buyer asks to increase the insurance premium or scope of risks, he should get the permission of the Seller before time of loading, and all the charges thus incurred should be borne by the Buyer.

15. Quality/Quantity Discrepancy: In case of quality discrepancy, claim should be filed by the Buyer within 30 days after the arrival of the goods at port of destination; while for quantity discrepancy, claim should be filed by the Buyer within 15 days after the arrival of the goods at port of destination. It is understood that the Seller shall not be liable for any discrepancy of the goods shipped due to causes for which the Insurance Company, Shipping Company, other transportation organizations and/or Post Office are liable.

16. The Seller shall not be held liable for failure or delay in delivery of the entire lot or a portion of the goods under this Sales Contract in consequence of any Force Majeure incidents.

17. Arbitration: All disputes in connection with this contract or the execution thereof shall be settled friendly through negotiations. In case no settlement can be reached, the case may then be submitted for arbitration to China International Economic and Trade Arbitration Commission in accordance with the provisional Rules of Procedures promulgated by the said Arbitration Commission. The arbitration shall take place in Beijing and the decision of the Arbitration Commission shall be final and binding upon both parties; neither party shall seek recourse to a law court nor other authorities to appeal for revision of the decision. Arbitration fee shall be borne by the losing party. Or arbitration may be settled in the third country mutually agreed upon by both parties.

II Fill in the contract form in English with the particulars given in the following letter.

2015年11月5日中国化工进出口总公司与新加坡 Smith & Son's Co., Ltd. 在北京签订了第 CE113 号合同。中国化工进出口总公司向 Smith & Son's Co., Ltd. 出售 50 公吨锌钡白（Lithophone），其硫化锌（ZnS）含量不得低于 28%。合同要求用内衬纸袋的玻璃纤维（glass-fibre）袋装。货物于 2016 年 1 月自天津新港装船运往新加坡，允许分批装运和转船。合同的其他主要内容如下：买方允许卖方5%的溢短装，价格仍按单价计算；单价为CIF新加坡每公吨人民币1 000元含佣3%；支付条件为由买方通过卖方接受的银行于装运前30天开立并送达卖方不可撤销的即期信用证，至装运后15天在中国议付有效；保险由卖方根据中国人民保险公司海洋货物运输条款按发票总值的110%投保一切险和战争险，如买方欲增加其他险别或超过上述保额时，须于装船前征得卖方同意，所增加的保险费有买方负担。

SELLERS：
BUYERS：

This Contract is made by and between the Buyers and the Sellers agree to sell the undermentioned commodity according to the terms and conditions stipulated below：

Commodity：

Specifications：

Quantity：

Unit Price：

Total Value：

Packing：

Shipping Mark：

Insurance：

Time of Shipment：

Ⅲ Translate the following contract into English.

国际销售独家代理协议

本协议系于_____年_____月_____日，由当事人一方ABC公司，按中国法律组建并存在的公司，其主营业地在_____（以下简称卖方），与他方当事人XYZ

公司，按_____国法律组建并存在的公司，其主营业地在_____（以下简称代理商）所签订。

双方一致同意约定如下：

第一条　委任与接受

在本协议有效期内，卖方指定代理商为本协议第四条项下商品的独家代理商，在第三条所规定的区域内招揽顾客的订单。代理商同意并接受上述委任。

第二条　代理商的义务

代理商应严格遵守卖方随时给予的任何指令，而且不得代表卖方做出任何担保、承诺及订立契约、合同或做出其他对卖方有约束力的行为。对于代理商违反卖方指令或超出指令范围所有的一切作为或不作为，卖方都将不承担任何责任。

第三条　代理区域

本协议所指的代理区域是：_____（以下简称区域）。

第四条　代理商品

本协议所指的代理商品是：_____（以下简称商品）。

第五条　独家代理权

基于本协议授予的独家代理权，卖方不得在代理区域内，直接地或间接地，通过其他渠道销售、出口代理商品。代理商也不得在代理区域内经销、分销或促销与代理商品相似或有竞争性的商品，也不能招揽或接受以到区域外销售为目的的订单。在本协议有效期内，对来自于区域内其他顾客有关代理商品的订单、询价，卖方都应将其转交给代理商。

第六条　最低代理额和价格

在本协议有效期内，如果卖方通过代理商每年（12个月）从顾客处收到的货款总金额低于_____，则卖方有权提前30天书面通知代理商解除本协议。

卖方应经常向代理商提供最低的价格表及商品可以成交的条款、条件。

第七条　订单的处理

在招揽订单时，代理商应将卖方成交的条件、合同的一般条款充分通知顾客，也应告知顾客任何合同的订立都须经卖方的确认。代理商应将其收到的订单立即转交给卖方，以供卖方选择是否接受订单。卖方有权利拒绝履行或接受代理商所获得的订单或订单的一部分，而代理商对于被拒绝的订单或其中的一部分，无任何佣金请求权。

第八条　费用分担

除另有约定外，所有的费用和支出，如电讯费、差旅费及其他有关商品销售的费用，都应由代理商承担。除此以外，代理商还应承担维持其办公处所、销售人员及用于执行协议中有关代理商的义务而发生的费用。

第九条　佣金

卖方接受代理商直接获得的所有订单后，就应按商品净销售额的百分之_____，以_____（货币）支付给代理商佣金。佣金只有在卖方收到顾客的全部货款后，每6个月支付一次，以汇付方式支付。

第十条　商情报告

卖方和代理商都应按季度或按对方要求提供有关市场信息的报告，以尽可能促进商品的销售。代理商应向卖方报告商品的库存情况、市场状况及其他商业活动。

第十一条　商品的推销

在代理区域内，代理商应积极地、充分地进行广告宣传，以促进商品的销售。卖方应向代理商提供一定数量的广告印刷品、商品样本、小册子及代理商合理要求的其他材料。

第十二条　工业权保护

在本协议有效期内，代理商可使用卖方的商标，但仅限于代理商品的销售。如果在本协议终止后，代理商在销售库存代理商品时，仍可使用卖方的商标。代理商也承认使用于或包含于代理商品中的任何专利、商标、版权及其他工业产权，都属于卖方所有，并且不得以任何方式提出异议。一旦发现侵权，代理商应及时通知卖方并协助卖方采取措施保护卖方产权利益。

第十三条　协议期限

本协议经双方签字生效。在本协议终止前至少3个月，卖方或代理商应共同协商协议的续延。如果双方一致同意续延，在上述规定的条款、条件下，附上补充文件，本协议将继续有效另外＿＿＿＿年。发生续延，本协议将于＿＿＿＿年＿＿＿＿月＿＿＿＿日终止。

第十四条　协议的中止

在本协议有效期内，任何一方当事人不履行合同或违反本协议的条款，如第五、六、十一条，双方当事人争取及时解决争议的问题，以期双方满意。如果在违约方接到书面通知后30日内问题仍不能解决，非违约方将有权中止本协议，由此造成的损失由违约方承担。如一方出现破产、无力偿付债务、清算、死亡或被第三方兼并，另一方可提出中止本协议，而无需书面通知对方。

第十五条　不可抗力

任何一方对由于下列原因而导致不能或暂时不能履行全部或部分协议义务的，不负责任：自然灾害、政府采购或禁令及其他任何双方在签约时不能预料、无法控制且不能避免和克服的事件。但受不可抗力影响的一方，应尽快地将发生的事件通知对方，并附上证明材料。

第十六条　准据法

本协议有关贸易条款应按INCOTERMS 2010解释。本协议的有效性、组成及履行受中华人民共和国法律管辖。

第十七条　仲裁

对于因履行本协议发生的一切争议，双方应友好协商解决，如协商无法解决争议，则应提交中国国际经济贸易仲裁委员会仲裁，依据其仲裁规则，仲裁费应由败诉一方承担，仲裁委员会另有规定的除外。

本协议由双方代表签字后生效，一式两份，双方各执一份。

ABC 公司　　　　　　　　　　　　　　　　　　　　　　XYZ 公司
代表：＿＿＿＿＿＿　　　　　　　　　　　　　　　　　代表：＿＿＿＿＿＿

IV Translate the following Articles into Chinese.

Part II Formation of the Contract

Article 14

(1) A proposal for concluding a contract addressed to one or more specific persons constitutes an offer if it is sufficiently definite and indicates the intention of the offeror to be bound in case of acceptance. A proposal is sufficiently definite if it indicates the goods and expressly or implicitly fixes or makes provision for determining the quantity and the price.

(2) A proposal other than one addressed to one or more specific person is to be considered merely as an invitation to make offers, unless the contrary is clearly indicated by the person making the proposal.

Article 15

(1) An offer becomes effective when it reaches the offeree.

(2) An offer, even if it is irrevocable, may be withdrawn if the withdrawal reaches the offer before or at the same time as the offer.

Article 16

(1) Until a contract is concluded an offer may be revoked if the revocation reaches the offeree before he has dispatched an acceptance.

(2) However, an offer cannot be revoked:
   (a) if it indicates, whether by stating a fixed time for acceptance or otherwise, that it is irrevocable; or
   (b) if it was reasonable for the offeree to rely on the offer as being irrevocable and the offeree has acted in reliance on the offer.

Article 17

An offer, even if it is irrevocable, is terminated when a rejection reaches the offeror.

Article 18

(1) A statement made by or other conduct of the offeree indicating assent to an offer is an acceptance. Silence or inactivity does not in itself amount to acceptance.

(2) An acceptance of an offer becomes effective at the moment the indication of assent reaches the offeror. An acceptance is not effective if the indication of assent does not reach the offeror within the time he has fixed or, if no time is fixed, within a reasonable time, due account being taken of the circumstances of the transaction, including the rapidity of the means of communication employed by the offeror. An oral offer must be accepted immediately unless the circumstances indicate otherwise.

(3) However, if, by virtue of the offer or as a result of practices which the parties have established between themselves or of usage, the offeree may indicate assent by performing

an act, such as one relating to the dispatch of the goods or payment of the price, without notice to the offeror, the acceptance is effective at the moment the act is performed, provided that the act is performed within the period of time laid down in the preceding paragraph.

Appendix A

Useful Abbreviations in International Trade

实用国际贸易缩略语

a/c bk.	account book	账本
a/c pay	account payable	应付账款
a/c rec.	account receivable	应收账款
A. O.	account of	……账上
A/R	all risks	一切险，全险
A/V	ad valorem	按价，从价
acct.	account	账目
ad. loc.	to (or at) the place	到或在当地
add.	address	地址
admin.	administration	行政
adv. /advt.	advertisement	广告
agr.	agriculture	农业
agt.	agent	代理商
amt.	amount	金额
AR	account receivable	应收账
assoc.	association	协会
asst.	assistant	助理
atty.	attorney	代理
attn.	attention	经办
av.	average	平均，海损
bal	balance	余额
barg	bargain	谈判
B. N.	banknote	银行存折
BBA	Bachelor of Business Administration	工商管理学士
B. C.	bank clearing	清算
B. D.	bank draft	银行汇票
B. E.	bill of exchange	汇票

Appendix A Useful Abbreviations in International Trade

b. o.	buyer's option	买方选择
B. S.	balance sheet	资产负债表
B/E	bill of exchange	汇票
B/L	bill of lading	提单
B/P	bills payable	应付票据
bkpg.	bookkeeping	簿记
bkpt.	bankrupt	破产
bl.	barrel	大桶
C. A. D.	cash against documents	凭票付款
C&F	cost and freight	成本加运费
C. B. D.	cash before delivery	付现后交货
c. c.	carbon copy	抄送，副本，印送
c. d.	cash discount	现付折扣
CIF	cost, insurance, and freight	成本加保险加运费价
CPA	certified public accountant	注册会计师
c. w. o.	cash with order	订货付现
C/N	credit note	付款清单，贷项通知
c/o	care of	由……转交
cert.	certificate	证书
cf.	compare	参见
c/f	carried forward	转下页
cml.	commercial	商务的，电视广告
co.	company	公司
COD	cash on delivery	货到付款
cons.	consignment	寄售
corp.	corporation	公司
c. o. s.	cash on shipment	装船付现
cr.	credit	贷方，信贷，赊账
ctn.	carton	纸箱
D/A	days against acceptance	承兑后若干日付款
DAS	delivered alongside ship	船边交货
dpt.	department	系，部门
disc.	discount	折扣
div.	dividend	股息，股利
divy.	delivery	交货
doz.	dozen	打，十二个
dup.	duplicate	副本，抄件
EAT	earning after tax	税后净利
EB	export bounty	出口补贴

EBB	extra best best	特级质量
e. g.	for example	例如
enc., encl.	enclosed or enclosure	附上，附件
et al.	and other (Latin *et alii*)	以及，其他，等等
etc.	and so forth	等等
ex. ship	delivered out of ship	在目的地港船上交货
F	finance	金融
FA	forwarding agent	货运承运人
FAA	free of all average	一切海损均不赔偿
FAS	free alongside ship	船边交货价
FB	freight bill	运费单
FOB	free on board	船上交货价
FOC	free of charge	免费
FOD	free of damage	损坏不赔
FPA	free of particular average	平安险
ft	foot	英尺
G/A	general average	共同海损
GAP	gross agriculture product	农业生产总值
GNP	gross national product	国民生产总值
GPT	general preferential tariff	普通优惠税
GR	grade	等级
ha	hectare	公顷
hdqrs.	headquarters	总部
hp	horsepower	马力
hr	hour	小时
ht	height	高度
IC	inspected and condemned	检验并报废
Id	idem	同前
i. e.	that is (Latin *id est*)	即
in trans.	in transit	在运输中
in.	inch	英寸
ins.	insurance	保险
int.	interest	利息
inv.	invoice	发票
J/A	joint account	共同账户
K	kilogramme	公斤
K. N.	kilogramme net weight	公斤净重
L/C	letter of credit	信用证
Ltd.	limited	有限公司

Appendix A Useful Abbreviations in International Trade

l. w. t.	landing weight	卸货重量
MA	market analysis	市场分析
M. A. P.	maximum average price	最高平均价格
Mart.	market	市场
m. b.	merchant broker	商业经纪人
MBA	Master of Business Administration	工商管理硕士
MIP	marine insurance policy	海运保险单
M. O.	money order	汇款单
M. T.	metric ton	公吨
max.	maximum	最大额
Messrs.	Messieurs	Mr.的复数
mgte.	Mortgage	抵押
min.	minimum	最小额
mkt.	market	市场
m. p. h.	miles per hour	英里/小时
N. A.	net value	净值
n. b. /N. B.	note carefully	注意，留心
N. E.	no effect	无效
NFS	not for sale	非卖品
N. N. P.	net national product	国民生产净值
O/A	on account	欠账
O. B/L	order bill of lading	指示提单
O. D.	on demand	见票即付
Off.	offered	开价
O. G.	ordinary goods	普通货物
OLT	overland transportation	陆路运输
O/N	order notify	订单通知
o. r. b.	owner's risk of breakage	货主负担破损险
o. s., O/S	out of stock	无存货
oz	ounce	盎司
patt.	patent	专利
P. B.	pass book	银行存折
PBC	People's Bank of China	中国人民银行
p. b. t.	profit before tax	税前利润
P. C.	paid cash	支付现款
Pcl.	parcel	包裹
PCT	prime contract termination	原合同终止
P. L.	partial loss	部分损失
P. O. E.	port of entry	进口港，海关港

p. p., P. P.	parcel post	邮寄包裹
P. S.	post script	附言
pat.	patent	专利
payt., p. t.	payment	付款
pd.	paid	已付
per ann.	per annum	每年
pkg.	package	包装
ppd.	post paid	邮费已付
PR	public relations	公关
R. O. D.	receipt of goods	交货收据
R. S. V. P.	please reply	请答复
Re.	concerning, in reference to	关于
rat	ration	定额
R. B.	receipt book	收据本
R. B. N.	registry of business names	商标注册处
R. C.	reimbursement credit	偿付信用证
Rcpt	receipt	收据
r. d.	running days	连续工作日
R/E	refer to endorser	请询背书人
rec.	reclaimation	要求赔偿损失
recd.	received	收到
S	stock	股票
S. A.	savings account	存款账户
S/A	subject to approval	有待批准
S&C	shipper and carrier	托运人与承运人
S/C	sales confirmation	销售确认书
S. C. I.	special customs invoices	海关特别发票
S. D.	special delivery	邮政专递
shpt.	shipment	装船
T	table	表格
t. a.	time of arrival	到达时间
tal	total	总计
tar	tariff	关税
tax	taxation	征税
T. B. L.	through bill of lading	联运提单
TC	tariff ceiling	关税最高限额
Tfc Vol	traffic volume	运输量
T. L.	time loan	定期贷款
T. O.	turnover	成交额

Appendix A Useful Abbreviations in International Trade

T. T.	telegraphic transfer	电汇
V. A. T.	value-added tax	增值税
V. P.	vice president	副总裁
W. A.	with average	水渍险
W. B.	waybill	运货单
W. P. A.	with particular average	水渍险

Appendix B

Useful Expressions in INCOTERMS 2010 and the Relevant Documents
《2010 年国际贸易术语解释通则》及相关文件中的实用表达

1. 贸易术语

INCOTERMS (International Commercial Terms)/International Chamber of Commerce International Rules for the interpretation of Trade Terms　国际商会国际贸易术语解释通则

Trade terms/price terms　贸易术语

CIF（Cost, Insurance & Freight）　成本、保险加运费付至（...指定目的港）

CIF Liner Terms　成本加运保费价（班轮条件）

CIF Ex Ship's Hold　成本加运保费价、卸货费

CFR（Cost & Freight）　成本加运保费价

CFR Landed　成本加运费、卸货费

CPT（Carriage Paid to）　运费付至（...指定目的港）

DIP（Carriage, Insurance Paid to）　运费、保险费付至（...指定目的地）

DAT（Delivered at Terminal）　终点站交货（...指定目的港或目的地）

DAP（Delivered at Place）　目的地交货（...指定目的地）

DDP（Delivered Duty Paid）　完税后交货（...指定目的地）

EXW（Ex Works）　工厂交货（...指定地点）

FAS（Free Alongside Ship）　船边交货（...指定装运港）

FCA（Free Carrier）　货交承运人（...指定地点）

FOB（Free on Board）　船上交货（...指定装运港）

FOB Liner Terms　装运港船上交货价（班轮条件）

FOB Under Tackle　装运港吊钩下交货

FOB Stowed　包括理舱费在内的装运港船上交货价

Appendix B Useful Expressions in INCOTERMS 2010 and the Relevant Documents

FOB Trimmed　包括平舱费在内的装运港船上交货价
FOBST（FOB Stowed & Trimmed）　包括理舱费、平舱费在内的装运港船上交货价

2. 组织机构

Asian Development Bank　亚洲发展银行
Bank of Communications　交通银行
Bank of China　中国银行
Industrial and Commercial Bank of China　中国工商银行
China Merchants Bank　招商银行
China Construction Bank　中国建设银行
China Agricultural Bank　中国农业银行
CCIB（China Commodity Inspection Bureau）　中国商品检验局
CCPIT（China Council for the Promotion of International Trade）　中国国际贸易促进委员会
EU（European Union）　欧盟
International Chamber of Commerce　国际商会
International Bank for Settlement　国际清算银行，国际结算银行
IMF（International Monetary fund）　国际货币基金组织
ISO（International Standard Organization）　国际标准化组织
OECD（Organization of Economic Cooperation and Development）　经济合作和发展组织
OPEC（Organization of Petroleum Exporting Countries）　石油输出国组织
UNCTAD（Unite Nations Conference on Trade & Development）　联合国贸易与发展会议
UNDP（United Nations Development Program）　联合国开发计划署
WTO（World Trade Organization）　世界贸易组织

3. 货币

AUD（Australian Dollar）　澳大利亚元
CNY（Renminbi Yuan）　人民币元
CAD（Canadian Dollar）　加拿大元
EGP（Egyptian Pound）　埃及镑
EUR（Euro）　欧元
GBP（Great British Pound Sterling）　英国英镑
GRD（Greek Drachma）　希腊德拉马克

HKD（Hong Kong Dollars） 港币
ITL（Italian Lira） 意大利里拉
INR（Indian Rupee） 印度卢比
JPY（Japanese Yen） 日圆
KPW（Korean Won） 朝鲜圆
MXP（Mexican Peso） 墨西哥比索
MOP（Macao Pataca） 澳门澳元
NZD（New Zealand Dollar） 新西兰元
USD（U. S. Dollar） 美元
VND（Vietnamese Dong） 越南盾
SJD（Singapore Dollar） 新加坡元
SUR（Russian Ruble） 俄罗斯卢布
THP（Thai Baht） 泰铢
ZAR（South African Rand） 南非兰特

4. 价格

agreement price 商议价
base price 基价
competitive price 具有竞争力的价格
contracted price 合同所列的价格
cost price 成本价
dumping price 倾销价
estimated price 预计价
forward price 期货价
feasible price 可行的价格
favorable price 优惠价
monopoly price 垄断价
moderate price 适中的价格
net price 净价
nominal price 名义价格
price adjustment 价格调整
reference price 参考价格
reasonable price 合理价格
spot price 现货价
suitable price 合适的价格
unit price 单价
total price, total value, total amount 总价

retail price 零售价
wholesale price 批发价

5. 付款

acceptance 承兑
accept draft 承兑汇票
advance payment guarantee 预付款担保函
anticipatory L/C 预支信用证
applicant（开证） 申请人
advising bank, notifying bank 通知行
bona fide holder 善意/正当持票人
beneficiary 受益人
bill of exchange, draft 汇票
banker's draft 银行汇票
back to back L/C 背对背信用证
bank guarantee for loan 借款担保函
CAD (Cash against Documents) 凭单付现
check, cheque 支票
collection 托收
cash with order 订单付款
confirmed letter of credit 保兑信用证
commercial draft 商业承兑汇票
confirming bank 保兑行
D/D (remittance by banker's Demand Draft) 票汇
documentary credit 跟单汇票
deferred payment 延期汇票
drawee 受票人
drawer 出票人
deposit 押金
D/A (Documents against Acceptance) 承兑交单
documentary L/C 跟单信用证
dishonor 拒付
documentary bill 托付
down payment 预付定金
D/P (Documents against Payment) 付款交单
D/P at sight 即期付款交单
D/P after sight 远期付款交单

endorsement 背书
endorser 背书人
irrevocable letter of credit 不可撤销信用证
L/C (Letter of Credit) 信用证
letter of guarantee 担保函,保函
money order 汇款单
M/T (mail transfer) 信汇
non-transferable L/C 不可转让信用证
negotiating bank 议付行
opening bank, issuing bank 开证行
partial payment credit 部分预付信用证
payer 付款人
payee 受款人
presenting bank 提示行
paying bank, drawee bank 付款行
payment in advance 预付
payment by installments 分期付款
performance guarantee 履约保函
presentation 提示（汇票等）
principal 委托人
promissory note 本票
reciprocal credit 对开信用证
remittance 汇付
remitting bank 汇付行
repayment guarantee 偿付担保书
revocable L/C 可撤销信用证
revolving L/C 循环信用证
standby L/C 备用信用证
sight L/C 即期信用证
sight draft 即期汇票
T/T (trust receipt) 信托收据
time draft/usance draft/term draft 远期汇票
usance credit payable at sight L/C 假远期信用证
usance L/C, time L/C 远期信用证
UCP 600 跟单信用证统一惯例（600号出版物）

6. 商务谈判与合同

allowance 折上，减价，补贴
bid 出价，递盘
bargain 讨价还价
conditional acceptance 有条件接受
commission 佣金
contract 合同
counter offer 还盘
discount 折扣，贴现
firm offer 实盘
inquiry note 询价单
inquiry, enquiry 询价，询盘
invitation to offer 邀请发盘
modification （发盘的）修改
non-firm offer 虚盘
offer 报盘
offerer 发盘人
offeree 受盘人
offer without engagement 不具约束力的报盘
order 订单
product list 货单
price list 价格单，价目表
purchase contract 购货合同
purchase confirmation 购货确认书
purchase note 购货单
quotation 报价
quotation sheet 报价单
rebate 回扣
sales contract 销售合同
sales note 售单
sales confirmation 销售确认书
sign a contract 签署合同
trade agreement 贸易协议
voluntary offer 主动发盘
withdrawal （发盘的）撤回

7. 货物质量，重量和尺码

article number（Art No.） 货号
counter sample 回样，对等样品
conditional weight 公量
description of goods 品名
detailed specifications 详细的规格
FAQ（Fair Average Quality） 大路货，中等平均品质
grade of goods 货物等级
gross weight 毛重
gross for net 以毛作净
legal weight 法定重量
long ton 长吨
measurement ton 尺码吨
metric ton 公吨
model number, type number 型号
net weight 净重
name of commodities 品名
quality as per seller's sample 质量以卖方样品为准
quality as per buyer's sample 质量以买方样品为准
sale by descriptions and illustrations 凭说明书和图样买卖
pattern number 花型号
sale by grade 凭等级买卖
sale by specification 凭规格买卖
sale by standard 凭标准买卖
sample order 凭样品订货
specifications of goods 货物的规格
short ton 短吨

8. 运输

airway transport 航空运输
consignment 托运物，运输
consignor, shipper 发货人，托运人
consignee 收货人
container transport 集装箱运输

Appendix B Useful Expressions in INCOTERMS 2010 and the Relevant Documents

calling port　停靠港
direct steamer　直达船
demurrage (money, fee, charge)　滞期费
dispatch money　速遣费
EMP (European Main Port)　欧洲主要港口
freight　运费
freight forwarder, forwarding agent　货运代理人
freight to collect, freight to be paid　运费到付
freight prepaid, freight paid　运费已付
land bridge, continental bridge　大陆桥
inland water transportation　内河航运
international combined transport　国际联运
intermodal transport, multimodal transport　多式联运
liner's transport　班轮运输
lay time　装卸时间
notify party　被通知人
ocean transport, marine transport　海洋运输
optional port　选择港
parcel post transport　邮包运输
port of destination　目的港
port of transshipment　转运港
port of loading, port of shipment　装运港
partial shipment　分批装运
port surcharge　港口附加费
port congestion surcharge　港口拥堵附加费
rail transport　铁路运输
road transportation　公路运输
shipping marks　装运标志
shipping advice　装运通知
shipping instructions　装运须知
shipping space　舱位
shipping documents　装运单据
transshipment　转运
tramp　不定期租船
time charter　期租船
voyage charter　程租船
weight ton　重量吨
weather working days　晴天工作日

9. 包装

commercial packing　商业包装
customary packing, usual packing　习惯包装
conventional export packing　传统出口包装
designated packing　指定包装
export standard packing　出口标准包装
export packing　出口包装
indicative mark　指示性标志
in bulk　散装
inner packing　内包装
marketing packing　销售包装
neutral packing　中性包装
nude packed　裸包装
outer packing　外包装
official marks　官方规定标志
packing cost　包装成本
packing charges/expenses　包装费
packing material　包装材料
packing specifications　包装规格
seaworthy packing　适航运输包装
stencil shipping marks　唰唛头
waterproof packing　防水包装
warning mark　警告性标志

10. 保险

accident　意外事故
average　海损
actual total loss　实际全损
All Risks　一切险
additional risks　附加险
constructive total loss　推定全损
CIC (China Insurance Clause)　中国保险条款
Damage Caused by Heating and Sweating　受热受潮险
extraneous risks　外来风险

Appendix B Useful Expressions in INCOTERMS 2010 and the Relevant Documents

franchise 相对免赔额
FPA (Free from Particular Average) 平安险
general additional risks 一般附加险
GA (General Average) 共同海损
Hook Damage 钩损险
ICC (Institute Cargo Clause) 协会货物保险条款
insurance 保险
insurer 保险商
insurance agent 保险代理人
insurance broker 保险经纪人
insurance company 保险公司
insurance coverage 投保范围
insurance claim 保险索赔
Open Policy 预约保单
Ocean Maritime Cargo Clauses 海洋运输货物保险条款
partial loss 部分损失
PA (Particular Average) 单独海损
premium 保险费
PICC (People's Insurance Company of China) 中国人民保险公司
Risk of Odor 串味险
Risk of Rust 锈损险
Risk of Leakage 渗漏险
Risk of Clash and Breakage 破损破碎险
Risk of Shortage 短量险
salvage charges 救助费用
SRCC (Strikes, Riots & Civil Commotions) 罢工暴动民变险
special additional risks 特殊附加险
the insured 被保险人，投保人
total loss 全损
TPND (Theft, Pilferage & Non-Delivery) 偷窃和提货不着险
underwriter 保险商
WPA (With Particular Average), WA (With Average) 水渍险
War Risk 战争险
W/W (Warehouse to Warehouse) 仓至仓条款

11. 检验

Commodity Inspection Bureau 商品检验局
Disinfection Inspection Certificate 消毒检验证书

Inspection Certificate of Value　价值检验证书
Inspection Certificate of Quality　质量检验证书
Inspection Certificate of Health　卫生检验证书
Inspection Certificate of Origin　原产地检验证书
Inspection Certificate of Weight　重量检验证书
Inspection Certificate of Tank/Hold　验舱证书
Inspection Certificate of Loss or Damage　残损证书
Inspection Certificate of Damaged Cargo　验残检验证书
Veterinary Inspection Certificate　兽医检验证书

12. 索赔与仲裁

arbitration　仲裁
arbitral award　仲裁裁决
arbitration clause　仲裁条款
breach/violation of contract　违反合同
breach/violation of condition　违反要件
dispute　争执，纠纷
defendant　被诉方
discrepancy and claim clause　异议、索赔条款
fundamental breach　根本违反
force majeure　不可抗力
lodge a claim against sb.　向……提出索赔
minor breach　轻微违约
material breach　重大违约
penalty　罚金
settlement of claim　理赔

13. 单据

airway bill　空运单
bill of lading　提单
commercial invoice　商业发票
cargo receipt（承运）　货物收据
clean B/L　清洁提单
container B/L　集装箱提单

C. T. D. （combined transport documents） 多式联运提单
consular invoice 领事发票
customs invoice 海关发票
certificate of origin 原产地证
direct B/L 直达提单
insurance policy 保险单
insurance certificate 保险证书
liner B/L 班轮提单
order B/L 指示提单
original B/L 正本提单
on deck B/L 舱面提单
on board B/L 已装船提单
packing list 装箱单
railway bill 铁路运输
received for shipped B/L 受货备运提单
straight B/L 记名提单
stale B/L 过期提单
transshipment B/L 转船提单
unclean B/L, foul B/L 不清洁提单
weight memo 重量单

14. 贸易方式

agent 代理人
agency 代理行
auction 拍卖
bilateral trade 双边贸易
barter trade 易货贸易
bidder 竞买者
bidding 递盘
broker 经纪人
brokerage 经纪费
counter purchase 互购
counter trade 对销贸易
consignment terms 寄售方式
compensation trade 补偿贸易
distributor 分销商
exclusive sales 包销

exclusive agent, sole agent　独家代理
entrepot trade　转口贸易
futures exchange　期货交易所
futures trading, futures transaction　期货交易
forward contract　期货合同
hedging　套期保值
invitation to tender　招标
leasing trade　租赁贸易
multilateral trade　多边贸易
product buyback　产品回购
processing trade　加工贸易
processing of imported materials　来料加工
import/export quota　进口（出口）配额
sale by sample　凭样品销售
sealed bids, closed bids　密封递盘
submission to tender　投标

Appendix C

The Comparison of the Old and New Language Styles

新旧文体比较

旧文体	新文体
as per	as, according to ...
acknowledge receipt of	thank you for ..., I received ...
at an early date	soon, give a specific date
at this time, at present, at the present	now
adverting to your favour	appreciate your letter
Referring to attached hereto	attached, here or enclosed
beg	ask, request, hope
be in receipt of	thank you for ..., I received ...
due to the fact that	as, because or since
Enclosed please find	Enclosed is/are, here is/are
Herewith	here or omitted
I have before me	I am grateful for ...
take the liberty of	omitted
up to this writing	so far or omitted
Re. your letter	Appreciate your letter; Referring to your letter; Thank you for your letter
The writer wishes to acknowledge	Appreciate your letter; Referring to your letter; Thank you for your letter
We beg to thank you	Thank you
We beg to acknowledge	We have received
We beg to inform you	We are writing to inform you
We are in receipt of	Thank you for (your letter) or
The favour of your early reply will be obliged	We shall be glad to hear from you
Awaiting the favour of your early reply	We shall be glad to hear from you

take an early opportunity	Act promptly
take into consideration	Consider
It will be our constant aim	We shall try ...
This is to inform you of	We are pleased to tell you ...

繁琐文体   简约文体

繁琐文体	简约文体
at this time	now
come to a decision	decide
during the time that	while
express a preference for	prefer
due to the fact that	because
enclosed herewith	here
for the reason that	since (or: because)
for the purpose of	for (or: to)
from the point of view	as
in a position of	be able to
in all cases	always
in case	if
in due course	soon (or: in time)
in most cases	unusually
in accordance with your request	as you request
in compliance with your request	at your request
in spite of the fact that	although, even though
in order to	to
in regard to	regarding
in such a manner that	so
in the event that	if
in the neighborhood of	about
is in the process of	is
in other (some) cases	sometimes
in the amount of	for
in the matter of	about
in view of the fact that	because
in view of the foregoing	because, therefore
in (for) the amount of $500	for $500
in the city of New York	in New York
in the nature of	as

Appendix C The Comparison of the Old and New Language Styles

in the near future	soon
in connection with	by, in, for
in order to	regarding
inasmuch as	since
make inquiry regarding	inquire
make decision	decide
may rest assured	may be sure
on the grounds that	because
on the basis of	by
on behalf of	for
on the grounds of	because
pending receipt of	until
pertaining to	about
please forward	mail
pursuant to our agreement	as we agreed
reason is due to	because
under date of	dated
with due regards to	for, regarding
with (in) reference to	on, about
with (in) regard to	on, about
with (the) respect to	about
with the result that	so that
under separate cover	separately
during the year of 1999	during 1999
endorse on the back of this check	endorse this check
fulfill your order on this occasion.	present order.
for the price of $ 500	for $ 500
grateful and appreciative	grateful(or: appreciative)
It should be pointed out that	Please notice that
We would like benefit of	We need
We express our regret at being unable to	We are sorry we can't meet your
I want to take this opportunity to tell you	Thank you
That we are grateful to you	Please tell us
Please don't hesitate to tell us	Please
Will you be kind enough to	(Omitted the four wasted words)
Please be advised that	(Omitted the four wasted words)
This is to advise you	

References
参考文献

[1] BILBOW T G. Write for modern business. Beijing: Foreign Language Teaching and Research Press, 2001.

[2] BRUCE H, 张亦辉. High speed business writing. Beijing: Foreign Language Teaching and Research Press, 2006.

[3] 曹菱, 杨伶俐. 商务英语信函. 北京: 外语教学与研究出版社, 2000.

[4] 陈祥国, 刘启萍, 张晓玲, 等. 国际商务函电配套练习册. 北京: 中国商务出版社, 2004.

[5] 陈永生, 赵金仲, 陈晓鹏, 等. 国际商务与合同. 北京: 华语教学出版社, 2001.

[6] 程同春. 新编国际商务英语函电. 南京: 东南大学出版社, 2013.

[7] 葛萍. 外贸英语函电. 上海: 上海财经大学出版社, 2009.

[8] 范红. 英文商务写作教程. 北京: 清华大学出版社, 2004.

[9] 胡英坤, 车丽娟. 商务英语写作. 北京: 外语教学与研究出版社, 2013.

[10] 金双玉, 钦寅. 外贸英语函电与单证. 上海: 同济大学出版社, 2006.

[11] 兰天. 外贸英语函电. 大连: 东北财经大学出版社, 2012.

[12] 廖瑛, 陈楚君, 肖曼君, 等. 实用外贸英语函电. 武汉: 华中科技大学出版社, 2012.

[13] 戚云方. 外经贸英语函电与谈判. 杭州: 浙江大学出版社, 2007.

[14] 腾美荣. 外贸英语函电. 北京: 首都经济贸易大学出版社, 2011.

[15] 王兴孙, 张春鉷, 邬孝煜, 等. 新编进出口英语函电. 北京: 外语教学与研究出版社, 2012.

[16] 王素清. 国际商务写作教程. 北京: 对外经济贸易大学出版社, 1995.

[17] 王关富. 实用商务英语写作. 北京: 对外经济贸易大学出版社, 2008.

[18] 王兴懿. 商贸英语应用文大全. 北京: 机械工业出版社, 2004.

[19] 王丰, 陈沅沅. 国际商贸英语信函写作教程. 北京: 清华大学出版社, 2005.

[20] 王隆桂. 新英汉商务词典. 上海: 上海译文出版社, 2006.

[21] 万宁, 潘维琴, 陈双飞, 等. 外经贸英语函电. 北京: 机械工业出版社, 2006.

[22] 边毅. 商务英语写作. 修订本. 北京: 清华大学出版社; 北京交通大学出版社, 2006.

[23] 徐美荣. 新编外贸英语函电. 北京: 对外经济贸易大学出版社, 2011.

[24] 羡锡彪, 张佐成, 方春祥. 商务英语写作. 北京: 高等教育出版社, 2009.

[25] 尹小莹. 外贸英语函电. 西安: 西安交通大学出版社, 2012.

[26] 杨翠萍, 赵晓英, 程冰. 实用文秘英语文函. 西安: 西安交通大学出版社, 1999.

[27] 易露霞, 陈原. 实用英文商业信函. 广州: 广东经济出版社, 2004.

[28] 邹建华. 实用进出口英语函电. 北京: 电子工业出版社, 2005.

[29] 张春柏, 陈茂庆, 张锷, 等. 新编商务英语写作. 北京: 高等教育出版社, 2006.